Diving & Snorkeling
Cuba

Diana Williams

LONELY PLANET PUBLICATIONS
Melbourne • Oakland • London • Paris

Diving & Snorkeling Cuba
- A Lonely Planet Pisces Book

2nd Edition – October, 1999
1st Edition – 1996, Gulf Publishing Company

Published by
Lonely Planet Publications
192 Burwood Road, Hawthorn, Victoria 3122, Australia

Other offices
150 Linden Street, Oakland, California 94607, USA
10A Spring Place, London NW5 3BH, UK
1 rue du Dahomey, 75011 Paris, France

Photographs by photographers as indicated

Front cover photograph
Diver has a close encounter with a Nassau grouper and
yellowtail snappers near Isla de la Juventud,
by A. Nachoum

Back cover photographs
Graysby grouper and moray eel hide in the coral,
by U. Natoli
Sunset ride on Isla de la Juventud, by D. Williams
Divers explore the *Jibacoa* wreck, by U. Natoli

ISBN 0 86442 773 5

Printed by H&Y Printing Ltd., Hong Kong

**Although the author
and publisher have tried
to make the information
as accurate as possible,
they accept no responsi-
bility for any loss, injury
or inconvenience sus-
tained by any person
using this book.**

Contents

Author

L GOLDBERG

Diana Williams

Diana Williams lives near London and runs "Scuba en Cuba," a company specializing in diving and land tours of Cuba. She is currently working on a Ph.D. in Cuban tourism and has published several papers on tourism development. She is a qualified teacher and lecturer, and has traveled extensively through Asia, Australasia and Europe.

From the Author

This second edition would not have been possible without the help of some treasured people. A special "thank you" to all of them, particularly Bill Kerslake, Martina Speer, Barbara Azcuy, Brian Hernandez Azcuy, Lisbet Hernandez Azcuy, Guillermo Hernandez, Francisco Arazoza and Teresita Borges-Hernandez, as well as Jorge Mendez, Mary Martinez-Rizo, Vanessa Main and Louise Hirons from Cubanacán UK. Also Maritza Garrido and Jenny Granados from Cubanacán Viajes; everyone in the Puerto Sol offices in Havana; Pepe Omegna and Filippo Invernizzi from the Avalon Dive Center; Fidel Ferrer, Ernesto Cabrera and Frances Brown from Cubana de Aviación; Kate Eaton, Royer Alphonso Gamboa, Edward Hegney and all the dive guides that brought me to the beautiful dive sites described in this book. I would also like to thank those who helped me with the first edition (including Martina Speer, Ricardo Longo, Gustavo Gotera and Eduardo Nieto), and thus helped to get the ball rolling in the first place.

Contributing Photographers

An additional thanks to the photographers F. Arazoza, D. Dooley, L. Goldberg, G. Gotera, P. Harrison, W. Harrison, M. Keife, B. Kerslake, M. Lawrence, Dr. H.P. Mayer-Anhalt, A. Nachoum, U. Natoli, H. Poldervaart, S. Simonsen, E. Snijders and J. Webber, who have captured the spirit of Cuba and its colorful and vibrant marine world. Without their pictures, this book would not have been complete.

From the Publisher

The first edition of this book was published by Gulf Publishing Company. This second edition was published in Lonely Planet's U.S. office under the guidance of Roslyn Bullas, the "Divemaster" of Pisces Books. From the coral-encrusted Fish Tank, Sarah "Sunfish" Hawkins edited the text and photos and "Super Grouper" Emily Douglas designed the book and cover. Wendy "Wahoo" Smith and Deb "Dogfish" Miller provided ongoing editorial comments and encouragement. Navigating nautical charts were cartographers Patrick Bock, who created the maps, and Alex Guilbert, who supervised map production. Hayden Foell dove in to illustrate the underwater wreck and sidebar graphics.

Thanks also to the many others who contributed to this book: Bill Alevizon, for checking the marine life sections and technical sidebar text; Keith Bolender; Larry Clinton; Carlos Dell'Acqua; Larry Goldberg; and David Stanley. Portions of the text were adapted from Lonely Planet's *Cuba*.

Lonely Planet Pisces Books

Lonely Planet acquired the Pisces line of diving and snorkeling books in 1997. This series is being developed and substantially revamped over the next few years. We invite your comments and suggestions.

Pisces Pre-Dive Safety Guidelines

Before embarking on a scuba diving, skin diving or snorkeling trip, careful consideration should be given to the following to ensure a safe and enjoyable experience:

- Possess a current diving certification card from a recognized scuba diving instructional agency (if scuba diving)
- Be sure you are healthy and feel comfortable diving
- Obtain reliable information about physical and environmental conditions at the dive site (e.g., from a reputable local dive operation)
- Be aware of local laws, regulations and etiquette about marine life and environment
- Dive at sites within your experience level; if available, engage the services of a competent, professionally trained dive instructor or divemaster

Underwater conditions vary significantly from one region, or even site, to another. Seasonal changes can significantly alter any site and dive conditions. These differences influence the way divers dress for a dive and what diving techniques they use.

Regardless of location, there are special requirements for diving in that area. Before your dive, ask about the environmental characteristics that can affect your diving and how trained local divers deal with these considerations.

Warning & Request

Things change—dive site conditions, regulations, topside information. Nothing stays the same for long. Your feedback on this book will be used to update future editions and make the next edition more useful. Excerpts from your correspondence may appear in *Planet Talk*, our quarterly newsletter, or *Comet*, our monthly email newsletter. Please let us know if you don't want your letter published or your name acknowledged.

Correspondence can be addressed to:
Lonely Planet Publications
Pisces Books
150 Linden Street
Oakland, CA 94607
e-mail: pisces@lonelyplanet.com

Introduction

CUBANACÁN

Cuba offers excellent and varied diving suitable for divers and snorkelers of all ability levels and interests. The island's warm, clear waters are blessed with a diversity of marine life. It is not unusual to see rays, sharks, barracuda, grouper and many varieties of corals and sponges. You're likely to see schools of tropicals near the reefs, wrecks, walls, caves and canyons. In many areas it is possible to see several different features on a single dive. Most dives are easily reached via a short boat ride, and some can be accessed from the shore.

The "Diving in Cuba" section gives detailed descriptions of selected dive sites found in 12 of Cuba's most popular dive regions: María la Gorda; Isla de la Juventud; Cayo Largo; Playa Girón; Cienfuegos, Guajimico & Trinidad; Jardines de la Reina; Santiago de Cuba; Guardalavaca; Santa Lucía; Cayo Coco; Varadero; and the Havana Area. The sites described in this guide represent some of the best dive sites in each region.

The individual dive site descriptions provide specific information about the depth, accessibility and skill level of each dive to help you decide how well it suits

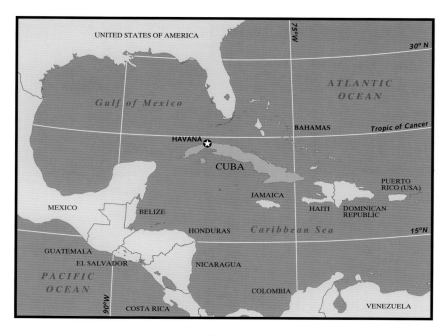

your abilities and interests and to help you determine your dive plan. Each site description also includes information about what marine life you can expect to see, and may suggest photography tips to help you get the best shot.

Even the most avid divers will want to spend some time on land. Several options are outlined in the "Activities & Attractions" section. "Practicalities" will help you plan for an enjoyable and comfortable trip no matter what activities you participate in.

A NACHOUM

It is possible, though uncommon, to spot schools of Atlantic spadefish in the open water off Cuba's Caribbean coast.

Overview

E SNIJDERS

Cuba is the largest island of the Greater Antilles, with an area of 110,860 sq km (42,803 sq miles). It is situated 180km (110 miles) south of the Florida Peninsula, just south of the Tropic of Cancer. The island's southern shore is bordered by the Caribbean Sea, and its northern coastline by the Atlantic Ocean. The country is composed of the main island of Cuba, Isla de la Juventud (Isle of Youth), and numerous archipelagos, cayes and islets. Its territory is divided into 14 provinces.

Cuba's rich culture is proudly displayed in cities such as Havana, Trinidad and Cienfuegos, which are famous for their colonial architecture, ornate churches and attractive squares. The island's long sandy beaches are perfect to use as a base for enjoying aquatic activities or just to relax. Its mountains provide ample opportunities for exploration of the natural environment.

Though political factors have prevented Cuba from being spoiled by mass consumerism, they have also inhibited the country's economic growth. While tourists enjoy the picturesque colonial towns, beautiful beaches, intriguing culture and rich history, many Cubans struggle to survive. The depressed economy has led to food and fuel shortages and regional blackouts, making daily life a struggle for most Cubans. Despite their hardships, the Cuban people are extremely friendly, welcoming tourists of all nationalities with their warm smiles.

History

Early Cuba

Christopher Columbus' arrival on Cuban shores in 1492 marked the meeting of Cuba's native cultures (Guanahatabey, Taino and Siboney) with the Europeans. The natives suffered through the resistance fighting, slavery and foreign diseases that eventually led to their demise. By the 16th century, few natives were left in Cuba, prompting the European colonists to import African slaves to work on cattle ranches and sugar, coffee and tobacco plantations.

D WILLIAMS

The Castillo de la Real Fuerza was completed in 1577.

Cuba became a Spanish protectorate in 1509. While in and out of Spanish hands, the sugar and tobacco industries expanded and the disparity in living conditions between wealthy plantation owners and slaves grew wider. Carlos Manuel de Céspedes, a progressive plantation owner, instigated a bitter rebellion on behalf of the slaves and slavery was abolished by 1888.

The Cuban Revolutionary Party was formed in 1892 with the goal of gaining financial support and weapons for Cuban and Puerto Rican independence. In 1895, Cuban exiles landed in Oriente (eastern Cuba) to fight the colonists. The Spanish reacted by imposing stricter controls. Tension continued and in 1898 the U.S. stepped in. On April 25, 1898, after Spain rejected the U.S. offer to buy Cuba for US$300 million, the U.S. declared war. Spain surrendered by July of that year, ending the Spanish-American war, fought on Cuban soil. By December, a peace treaty was signed.

U.S. influence increased in Cuba as U.S. corporations bought land, factories and railroads. Cuban resistance continued. The sugar crisis in the early 20th century did not encourage political harmony between the two countries.

Billboards in the Holguín area rally residents to fight for their country.

In the 1930s Fulgencio Batista began his rise to power. Staging a coup d'etat in 1952, Batista took control of Cuba by force. The first armed action against the coup took place in 1953, when Fidel Castro and his companions attacked the Moncarda barracks in Santiago de Cuba. The rebels were unsuccessful and Castro was captured a few days later.

In 1955, popular discontent led Batista to release the rebel group, which took exile in Mexico and continued to train and raise funds. In December 1956, Castro and a small army of revolutionaries returned to Cuba, intending to overthrow Batista. Only 12 of the expeditionaries survived the battle. In January 1957, the guerrillas scored their first success by overthrowing a small army outpost on the south coast. By December 1958, Castro occupied Oriente and Camagüey, later taking Santa Clara and Santiago de Cuba. On New Year's Day 1959, Batista fled the country. Castro had high public support when he took power that year.

El Comandante Gets Wet

Before the rest of the world discovered Cuba's reefs, they were enjoyed by a handful of Cubans, including El Comandante, Fidel Castro. In the '80s, Castro's favorite form of relaxation was to get together with a few *compañeros* at Cayo Piedra for fishing, followed by drinks and dinner. A modest four-room house on the caye was considered Fidel's real home at the time.

Though no longer an active diver, Castro's enthusiasm for diving was instrumental in the development of the diving industry in Cuba. His long-standing familiarity with Cuba's diving locales even led to his collaboration with Jacques Cousteau in the filming of *Cuba: Waters of Destiny*. Castro is quoted as saying, "I'm convinced that scuba diving is one of the most wonderful forms of recreation."

His interest in diving is so commonly acknowledged that—allegedly—several of the CIA's assassination plots hinged on this hobby. One scenario, planned during the Bay of Pigs hostage negotiations in 1961, involved giving Castro a dive suit dusted with a fungus that would produce a disabling and chronic foot disease. A second scenario involved getting Castro to pick up a particular shell while he was on one of his scheduled diving trips. The shell, loaded with explosives, would detonate when he examined it. Fortunately for Castro, there are few shells native to Cuban waters that are large enough to accommodate a lethal quantity of explosives.

– Larry Clinton

Post-Revolution

Cuba's isolation, a result of the revolution, forced it to look for an ally, which it found in the Soviet Union in 1960. Later that year Cuba declared itself communist. The U.S. quickly severed diplomatic relations with Cuba. The Soviet Union strengthened its Cuban ties by providing economic support.

Tension between the U.S. and Cuba grew. On April 17, 1961, 1,400 anti-Castro Cubans trained by the CIA landed at the Bahía de Cochinos (Bay of Pigs) in southern Cuba, intending to overthrow the government. The Cuban army thwarted the attack.

Further tension occurred in 1962 when the U.S. discovered the Soviet Union was building a military base in Cuba, complete with atomic weapons. The U.S. navy mobilized to intercept the missiles before they reached the island. After six intense days of discussion, Kruschev agreed to discontinue the project.

Political tensions between the U.S. and Cuba continue to influence U.S. policies, such as the economic embargo outlawing trade between the two countries. Most Soviet economic aid ended with the collapse of the Soviet Union in 1991. This, coupled with the U.S. embargo, has led to many shortages and economic problems for Cuba.

Recent events indicate a shift in international political support and economic policies for Cuba. In 1998, the United Nations General Assembly voted 157 to 2 to condemn the U.S. embargo against Cuba (12 delegates abstained). Relations between the U.S. and Cuba have improved somewhat—after the Pope's visit to Cuba in 1998, the U.S. reestablished air transport between Florida and Havana.

The Cuban government continues to support the growth of the tourism industry, which has strengthened its economy in recent years. In an effort to create a safe environment free of potential harassment, the government has cracked down on illegal activities; however, some tourists (particularly in Havana) feel this has dissuaded locals from interacting with tourists. Cuba's complex social and economic realities mean that the country is in a state of change: Policies are not always uniformly enforced and may change over time. Today Cuba's tourism industry continues to grow and improvements to the country's infrastructure and services are being made as the economy improves.

Geography

Forested mountains take up a quarter of Cuba's land, and fertile plains used for growing sugarcane and raising cattle account for a large part of the remaining land. The western Cordillera de Guaniguanico rises to almost 700m (2,300ft) and includes the Sierra de los Órganos and the Sierra del Rosario. The Sierra de Escambray is in central Cuba. To the east are the Sierra Maestra mountains, home of Cuba's highest point, Pico Turquino at 1,972m (6,470ft).

Cuba has approximately 8,000 species of flora, of which 45% are native, and is particularly known for its orchids, palms and pine trees. The national flower is the butterfly jasmine. Cuba's fauna is also rich, including 388 species of birds.

Cuba has nearly 6,000km (3,570 miles) of coastline and many sandy beaches. Its waters are home to 410 reported species of coral and sponges, and over 900 reported species of fish.

The 7,200m- (23,600ft-) deep Cayman trench, found between Cuba and Jamaica, forms the boundary of the Caribbean and North American tectonic plates and influences Cuba's southern marine topography. The Great Bahama Bank, located to the north between Cuba and the Bahamas, is much shallower. Tectonic activity has produced a varied coastline. The north and east coasts have limestone cliffs, while much of the southern coast is made up of low mangrove swamps. The same tectonic movements also created submerged valleys that now make good harbors, as seen in Cienfuegos and Santiago de Cuba.

E SNIJDERS

Havana Area
Wreck, wall and reef diving are found minutes from Cuba's historic capital city

Varadero
Several scuttled ships and a plane create a virtual divers' playground

Cayo Coco
Lush coral is home to large populations of tropicals around this pristine caye

Santa Lucía
Stingrays, spotted eagle rays and mantas grace deep dives and historic wrecks

Guardalavaca
Intimate beaches and scenic surroundings make this a favorite resort

Santiago de Cuba
Buttes, wrecks, caves and walls host abundant marine life

Playa Girón
Shore dive to swim-throughs and drop-offs in the infamous Bay of Pigs

Jardines de la Reina
Silky and blacktip sharks inhabit the waters of this remote archipelago

María la Gorda
The sheltered waters of this remote, pristine bay offer year-round diving

Isla de la Juventud
Great visibility and teeming marine life make this Cuba's most popular dive area

ATLANTIC OCEAN

Tropic of Cancer

BAHAMAS

NASSAU

FLORIDA (USA)

Gulf of Mexico

Tropic of Cancer

Province of Pinar del Río

Pinar del Río

Bauta

City of Havana

HAVANA

Province of Havana

Matanzas

Province of Matanzas

Nueva Gerona

Isla de la Juventud (Special Municipality)

Province of Cienfuegos

Cienfuegos

Santa Clara

Province of Villa Clara

Sancti Spíritus

Province of Sancti Spíritus

Ciego de Ávila

Province of Ciego de Ávila

Province of Camagüey

Camagüey

Las Tunas

Province of Las Tunas

Holguín

Province of Holguín

Guantánamo

Province of Guantánamo

HAITI

Bayamo

Province of Granma

Santiago de Cuba

Province of Santiago de Cuba

JAMAICA

KINGSTON

CAYMAN ISLANDS

Caribbean Sea

Cuba

Elevation
1500 m
1200 m
900 m
600 m
300 m
150 m
sea level

200 km
100 miles
100
50
0
0

24°N
22°N
20°N
18°N

84°W
82°W
80°W
78°W
76°W
74°W

Practicalities

B KERSLAKE

Climate

Cuba enjoys a pleasant subtropical climate with temperatures varying little throughout the year. Average air temperatures range between 26° and 32°C (79° and 90°F), with two seasons: the rainy season in the summer (May to October) and winter's dry season (November to April). Hurricanes can occur between June and November, with the worst storms usually arriving in September and October.

During the summer, mornings are generally sunny and humid, and some rain may fall for a short period in the afternoon. Air temperatures are around 30°C (86°F), though regional variations mean eastern Cuba is often hotter and more humid. Summer water temperatures average about 28°C (82°F).

The winter months are normally sunny and dry with average air temperatures around 26°C (79°F). Winter water temperatures average 24°C (75°F). The seas may be slightly rougher in winter, but diving is done year-round.

Culture

Cuba's diverse ethnic origins continue to play an important role in the island's culture. Though the native Guanahatabey, Siboney and Taino people were the first inhabitants of the island, they were almost entirely wiped out by the 16th century. Spaniards came to Cuba for the rich agricultural land, which was in short supply in their own country, and used the natives to work on plantations.

E SNIJDERS

With the depletion of the native population, the Spanish brought black slaves to Cuba from West Africa. A second influx of black workers was recruited from Haiti and Jamaica in the 1920s to work on Cuba's plantations and sugar fields.

People from Portugal, Italy, France and other countries also traveled to Cuba to set up residence. Chinese, many from

Macao and Canton, found their way to Cuban shores in the mid-1800s and worked as servants.

Today's Cuban culture—its people, religion, music and dance—is a blend of these many influences. Of Cuba's 11 million residents, 66% are white, 12% black and 22% are of mixed ancestry. Religious beliefs range from Catholic and Protestant faiths to Santería, which combines African deities with Catholic saints.

Language

Spanish is Cuba's official language and is spoken by all Cubans. Around the tourist resorts you are likely to hear English, Italian, German and French spoken by international visitors. English is a popular language to study and is spoken by many (though not always fluently) throughout the country. Up until 1991, Russian was also a common language to learn.

Getting There

About 40 airlines service Cuba. Most fly into José Martí International Airport in Havana from many European, Canadian and South and Central American cities. Some charter airlines fly into other tourist centers such as Varadero, Camagüey (the airport nearest Playa Santa Lucía) and Santiago de Cuba.

Diving & Flying

Divers in Cuba usually arrive by plane. While it's fine to dive soon *after* flying, it's important to remember that your last dive should be completed at least 12 hours (some experts advise 24 hours, particularly after repetitive dives), *before* your flight to minimize the risk of decompression sickness, caused by residual nitrogen in the blood.

Because travel between the U.S. and Cuba is severely restricted, U.S. citizens visiting Cuba normally enter by booking a pre-paid trip through a travel agent outside the U.S. Though there is a direct flight between Miami and Havana, it is normally used only by Cuban nationals, government officials, diplomats and their families, journalists and U.S. citizens with a Treasury Department license to visit Cuba.

Getting Around

On arrival, visitors on pre-booked tours will be met by a guide and taken to their destination by shuttle. For independent tourists, the easiest way to get to your destination is either by rented car or taxi. Cars can be rented at some airports and in the main cities, but because of increasing demand for rental cars, it is best to make reservations before arriving in Cuba through a travel agent or tour operator.

E SNIJDERS

A car is invaluable if you intend to see a lot of the island and are carrying heavy diving equipment. Cuba's road network is among the most highly developed in Latin America. Main roads are generally well maintained and roads outside of cities have little traffic. Driving is done on the right-hand side of the road.

Taxis are a good option for getting around large Cuban cities and can be hailed outside many hotels and airports. Taxi drivers in anything from a Lada to a '56 Chevrolet are eager to offer their transportation services.

D WILLIAMS
Cuban taxis come in all shapes and sizes.

Domestic flights are another good travel option. Flights operate between Havana and most major cities in Cuba: Nueva Gerona (Isla de la Juventud), Varadero, Ciego de Ávila (to access Jardines de la Reina), Cayo Coco, Camagüey (to access Santa Lucía), Bayamo, Holguín (to access Guardalavaca), Santiago de Cuba, Guantánamo and Baracoa. In addition, there are flights between Varadero and Cayo Coco, as well as between Holguín and Guardalavaca.

All of Cuba's provincial capitals are connected by railway. Though service is frequent, the trains are slow and often unreliable. That said, the service between Havana and Santiago de Cuba is reliable: The train departs late in the afternoon from Havana, arriving in Santiago some 14 hours later.

Buses are also available for long-distance journeys, but services tend to be limited and schedules unreliable. You can buy tickets in U.S. dollars at Havana's bus station.

Entry

Tourists must have a valid passport and a tourist card to enter Cuba. You should obtain your tourist card before you arrive. It can be issued through a (non-U.S.) travel agent, airline office or Cuban consulate. The card is valid for thirty days and can be renewed for up to six months at tourist offices in Cuba.

On arrival, your card is stamped by a customs officer who will also write in the length of time you wish to stay. The tourist card is removed from your passport upon departure. There is also a departure tax of about US$20.

Normally, tourists will be asked for proof of hotel reservations in the form of a voucher when they go through customs. If you have not made reservations beforehand, you may have limited (and very expensive) options.

Entry for U.S. Citizens

In conjunction with the U.S. embargo against Cuba, the U.S. government has prohibited its citizens from spending money in Cuba, effectively preventing travel. Enforcement of this law has fluctuated with the political climate.

The Helms-Burton Bill, signed in 1996, imposes (without judicial review) fines of up to US$50,000 on U.S. citizens who visit Cuba at their own expense without U.S.-government permission. The bill also allows for confiscation of violators' property. In addition, under the Trading with the Enemy Act, they may also face up to US$250,000 in fines and up to 10 years in prison. It is still unclear how this legislation will be implemented.

It is possible to arrange a pre-paid vacation with a non-U.S. (and non-Cuban) travel agency, thereby avoiding use of U.S. currency in Cuba. Most pre-paid trips enter Cuba via Canada, Mexico or the Bahamas. U.S. citizens should understand they are entering a "gray" area of the law using this method and are assuming the risk of possible legal action.

Cuban immigration officials know that a Cuban stamp in a U.S. passport can create problems, so when you hand over your passport to a Cuban immigration officer, be sure to request that it not be stamped. The officer will instead stamp your tourist card or a separate visa form that is collected as you leave Cuba.

Time

Cuba is on Eastern Standard Time, which is five hours behind GMT. When it is noon in Havana, it is 9am in San Francisco, 5pm in London and 4am (the following day) in Sydney. Cuba observes daylight saving time.

Money

Three currencies circulate in Cuba. The Cuban peso or *moneda nacional* is convenient for purchasing food in local restaurants or buying fruit, vegetables and souvenirs from street vendors, though you can't usually make major purchases (hotel accommodations, dive trips, etc.) with pesos. It is possible to exchange your currency for Cuban pesos at the small money-exchange offices found in major cities.

A more powerful currency is the U.S. dollar (also called *divisas*), which will buy almost anything. The *peso convertible* was introduced in 1994; it has the same value as the dollar.

Tipping in Cuba

Tipping is increasingly common, though not essential. If you feel well attended in a restaurant, for example, it is appropriate to tip the waiter (in US$) by rounding up your bill—though anyone in the service industry who goes out of their way to do you a special favor deserves a tip.

One tactic is to take both U.S. currency and traveler's checks. Credit cards like Visa and MasterCard issued through non-U.S. banks can also be used, although cards and traveler's checks linked to American Express will not be accepted.

Electricity

The most common current is 110 volts, 60 cycles, although some of the newer hotels operate on 220 volts, and some hotels have both. Check carefully before plugging in any electrical equipment. Bring a voltage converter, particularly if you need to recharge your camera lamp or strobe.

Though less of a problem in modern hotels, power outages, voltage drops and frequency fluctuations are still common. Don't plug in sensitive equipment such as portable computers if there is any doubt about a facility's electrical stability.

A plug adapter is also useful, if not necessary. Only a few of the newer hotels use the European-style outlets (two rounded pins). Most hotels use the American-style outlets (two flat prongs).

Weights & Measures

Cuba follows the metric system, though occasionally you'll hear references to American and Spanish measurements, such as an American gallon (3.785 liters), an *arroba* (25 Spanish pounds or 11.5kg) or a *vara* (an American yard or .91m). In this book, both metric and imperial measurements are given, except for specific references within a dive site description, which are given in metric units only.

What to Bring

General Supplies

The sun is strong in Cuba, so it is easy to get sunburned. Sun glasses and sun block are a must. A hat is also advisable.

Although you can buy toiletries in major cities, it is best to bring your own as options are limited and expensive. Traveling with a small stock of adhesive bandages, tampons, condoms, disinfectant, diarrhea pills, pain killers (such as aspirin or ibuprofen) and antihistamine tablets is advised. Mosquito repellent is a must.

Other items that you might consider bringing with you include a Spanish–English dictionary, a good map, a flashlight and batteries, film, pens, paper and reading material.

D WILLIAMS

Dive-Related Equipment

If you don't want to bring your own dive equipment, it is available for rent at most dive centers, though it is best to bring your own mask, fins and snorkel. On the whole, the quality of the dive equipment for rent is good. Prices can be negotiable, especially if you intend to rent dive equipment for a week or more.

If you plan to go night or cave diving, bring your own flashlight and batteries, which are often in short supply. Divers who bring their own DIN regulator should also bring an INT converting yolk, in case the dive operator does not have cylinders with DIN and INT connections. O-rings are also good to have on hand.

The water is warm—most divers do not normally need anything more than a 3mm wetsuit. Lycra suits are also good. In the hottest months it is possible to get by wearing just a t-shirt over your swimsuit.

Underwater Photography

Most dive centers do not have camera equipment for rent. If you want to take underwater photos and do not own a camera, consider renting one before leaving home. Bring your own silicone, as it can be difficult to find.

Though a variety of film is available, it is expensive, so it's better to bring film from home. If you want to process your film, the Photo-Servi shops found in most major cities process color print film, though serious photographers will want to develop their film at home.

Business Hours

Banks and exchange offices are open weekdays from 8:30am to noon and from 1:30 to 3pm. On Saturdays they are open from 8 to 10am, and they are closed on Sundays.

Post offices are generally open Monday-Saturday 8am to 6pm, though main post offices may stay open later.

Stores and offices tend to be open from 8:30am to 5:30pm. Some stay open continuously, while others will take a lunch break from 12:30 to 1:30pm.

Dive centers open around 9am to prepare for the morning dive. Dive schedules depend on the dive site. Typically, diving begins at 9:30am. Some dive centers close between the morning and afternoon dives for lunch.

Accommodations

Cuba has over 30,000 hotel rooms with more being added every year. You may be able to get a reservation in the basic, relatively cheap lodgings intended for Cubans, though the medium-priced hotels and expensive resorts are designed for foreign tourists. These accommodations invariably include air conditioning, private toilet and shower, a radio or television, a telephone and sometimes a refrigerator. Hotels that can cater to divers or that offer diving services tend to be moderately priced to expensive. Most visitors reserve accommodations through a tour operator or travel agent before arriving in Cuba.

It is also possible to stay in a Cuban home. The price for a room varies depending on whether you found the place on your own or were brought there by someone expecting a commission. As travel agents do not make this sort of arrangement, you will need to rely on recommendations from other travelers or the locals who offer their services to find a private room.

Dining & Food

Traditional Cuban cuisine includes rice and black beans (*morros y cristianos*) and (particularly in eastern Cuba) rice and kidney beans (*congrí*). Meat dishes include roast pork (which is traditional fare for New Year's celebrations), roast chicken and *ajiaco criollo*, a meat and vegetable stew. Grilled fish is found on many restaurant menus and lobster is often available.

Side dishes include *malanga* (sweet potato), *plátanos* (plantain bananas either fried or boiled), *yucca* (cassava) and salad. Popular desserts include the sweet, pink *guayaba* (guava), fruity *granizado* (a slushy fruit drink) and ice cream.

Cuba is famous for its cocktails, many of which are rum-based, including the *mojito* (fresh mint, sugar and rum), the *Cuba libre* (dark rum and Coke) and the daiquirí. Cuban beer (Mayabe, Cristal and Bucanero) is good, but wines tend to be somewhat limited. *Café cubano* is popular throughout Cuba and is served strong, in a small cup with lots of sugar. Another widely available Cuban drink is *guarapo* (sugarcane juice).

E SNIJDERS

Refreshment found in the form of a *granizado*.

Dining-out opportunities used to be largely limited to hotel restaurants. Now there is a wide range of restaurants and cafés, particularly in the larger cities and resorts. In Havana and Varadero you can find restaurants serving Cuban, Chinese, Italian and Spanish food. Havana even boasts its own health-food restaurant. Most restaurants and cafés are run by tourist companies, though the state does run restaurants that sell a limited range of food intended for peso-paying Cubans.

Hotel restaurants tend to serve a mix of traditional and international fare (with perhaps more emphasis on the international). A buffet breakfast (cheese, eggs, bacon, omelets, yogurt and fruit) is often included in your room price.

Another good option for eating out is the *paladares*. These small restaurants are often in the front room of a private home and serve traditional Cuban food.

Snacks like pizza and sandwiches are sold at a wide range of cafés. You can buy fruit and vegetables with pesos at small local markets.

To reduce your risk of digestive problems, it is best to drink bottled water and avoid drinks with ice. Eat fruits and vegetables that are peeled or thoroughly cooked. Hotels often serve canned vegetables, which are safe.

Shopping

The range of goods for sale, particularly handicrafts, has improved; however, Cuba is still not a shopping mecca. The most common tourist purchases are rum and cigars, for which Cuba is world famous. Coffee, dolls (linked to the Santería religion), different types of ornaments and paintings or prints also make good purchases.

In some of the larger markets you can find items such as black-coral jewelry, dried pufferfish, stuffed crocodiles, whole turtle shells and turtle-shell jewelry for sale. Buying items made from endangered animals such as these will only serve to enhance the threat to Cuba's natural and marine environments. Don't buy them!

Black Market Black Coral

The sale of black coral is managed by Cuba's Environmental Agency. According to the Decree Law 164, only 300kg (660lbs) of black coral can be extracted per year from Cuban waters for commercial purposes. Each piece of black-coral jewelry that is made must have a license and must be sold in specialized tourist shops. There are those who disregard the regulations, so real (as well as fake) black-coral jewelry can be found for sale in local markets. To preserve this valuable and beautiful resource, refrain from purchasing any black-coral products.

D WILLIAMS

Activities & Attractions

In addition to its underwater environment, Cuba has many historic, cultural and natural attractions. Imposing forts, colonial palaces, attractive squares and ornate churches are all reminders of its intriguing past. The island's rich ethnic mix has led to the development of a unique culture expressed through music, dance, art and religion.

Cuba's natural environment is also appealing. Rugged mountains, rolling hills, waterfalls, lush vegetation and extensive beaches provide enjoyable hiking and walking opportunities. While exploring, you are likely to see some of the indigenous species of birds, plants and animal life.

Havana

Havana, the capital city, is well worth a visit. The 1,170-sq-km (452-sq-mile) area is divided into 15 municipalities, two of which are of primary touristic importance: La Habana Vieja and Centro Habana.

La Habana Vieja, or "Old Havana" sits on the west side of the harbor in an area once bounded by 17th-century city walls. These walls were demolished in 1863, and the city spilled west into the area now called Centro Habana.

For a sense of Havana's rich past, spend some time walking the city's streets. Many of the older historic buildings have been restored and are now used as restaurants, cafés, bars and cultural centers. Don't miss the **Plaza de la Catedral**, which is flanked by a cathedral, museums and grand colonial palaces. The Restaurante El Patio, overlooking the square, is an excellent spot to take in the ambiance of this historic site and listen to live music.

Another site of interest is the **Plaza de Armas**, surrounded by buildings of historic importance. The **Museo de la Ciudad** (in the Palacio de los Capitanes Generales) has an impressive Baroque façade and stone pillars; it was the government seat until the 1790s. The plaza now serves as a market, where books, paintings and other souvenirs are sold.

Several forts merit a visit: the **Castillo de la Real Fuerza**, which is one of the oldest forts in the Americas, the **Castillo de los Tres Santos Reyes Magos del Morro** and nearby **Fortaleza de San Carlos de la Cabaña** act as guardians of Havana's bay. The latter is worth visiting not only for its architecture and historic importance, but also for its exhibitions. A reenactment of Spanish soldiers firing a cannon over Havana's bay occurs most nights at 9pm.

La Habana Vieja & Centro Habana

0   150   300 m
0   150   300 yards

Straits of Florida

To Playas del Este

Via Monumental

Castillo de los Tres Santos Reyes Magos del Morro

Entrance

Fortaleza de San Carlos de la Cabaña

Castillo de San Salvador de la Punta

Tunnel

Av Antonio Maceo (Malecón)

Parque de los Enamorados

Parque Mártires del 71

Av de los Estudiantes

Capdevila

San Lázaro

Av de Italia

Industria

Crespo

Consulado

Paseo de Martí

Genios

Morro

Colón

Refugio

Plaza 13 de Marzo

Av de las Misiones

Peña Pobre

Tacón

Cuarteles

Av Carlos Manuel de Céspedes

Parque Anfiteatro

Trocadero

Zulueta

Chacón

Tejadillo

Antiguo Palacio Presidencial

Parque Luz Caballero

Bernal

Amistad

Aguila

San Nicolás

Animas

Virtudes

Animas

Museo de Bellas Artes

Empedrado

San Juan de Dios

Parque Cervantes

Catedral de San Cristóbal de La Habana

Plaza de la Catedral

Castillo de la Real Fuerza

Plaza de Armas

Museo de la Ciudad

Baratillo

Justiz

Blanco

Neptuno

O'Reilly

Av de Bélgica

Obispo

Miguel

San Rafael

Parque Central

Obrapía

Mercaderes

Central Post Office

Rafael

Martín

San Martín

Casa de la Cultura Municipal

Plaza de San Francisco

Industria

Capitolio Nacional

Lamparilla

Plaza del Cristo

Amargura

Villegas

Aguacate

Compostela

Habana

Aguiar

Cuba

Oficios

San Ignacio

Plaza Vieja

Barcelona

Aguila

Amistad

Brasil

Cristo

Bernaza

Muralla

Santa Clara

Inquisidor

San Pedro

Dragones

Sol

Luz

Damas

Ferry

Muelle Luz

Ferry

Parque de la Fraternidad

Av Simón Bolívar

Máximo Gómez

Aramburu

Av de Bélgica

Picota

Acosta

Angeles

Rayo

Enrique Barnet (Estrella)

Corrales

Economía

Gloria

Misión

Jesús María

Merced

San Nicolás

Majola

Apodaca

Cárdenas

Cienfuegos

Conde

Leonor Pérez

Sitio

Factoría

Aponte

Arsenal

Parque de los Agrimensores

San Isidro

Velazco

Desamparados

Corrales

Suárez

Revillagigedo

Estación Central de Ferrocarriles

San Nicolás

Gloria

Florida

Aguila

Esperanza

Old City Wall

Bahía de La Habana

Figuras

Puerta Cerrada

Av de España

Diaria

Old Cars

You can't pass a busy street in Cuba without seeing a car from the 1940s or '50s (called *cacharros* or "old crocks" by the Cubans). Old Cadillacs, Chevys, Studebakers, De Sotos and Packards are everywhere—grand American cars that were imported before the U.S. trade embargo began in 1961.

You've got to admire the ingenious people who keep these cars on the road. Economic shortages mean that mechanics must often resort to using a mixture of shampoo, alcohol and brown sugar for brake fluid. A lack of spare parts means that Lada engines are used to replace worn out *cacharro* engines. Batteries are recharged from overhead power lines. These antique cars are mobile monuments to both the auto excesses of the past and the ingenuity nurtured by scarcity.

Music

Music is a big part of Cuban life, and you'll hear it everywhere—on the streets, in bars, in restaurants and in homes. Cuban music was called "a love affair between the African drum and the Spanish guitar" by ethnomusicologist Fernando Ortíz and its dances have become popular worldwide.

The *rumba*, which has African influences, developed in Cuba's black townships at the end of the 19th century. Its heady, pulsing beat is now famous throughout the world. String and brass instruments, brought to Cuba by the European settlers, were an important component to the development of ballads

Local musicians bring Havana to life at the Restaurante El Patio.

(*trovas*), which were sung accompanied by a guitar. In the dance halls, the *habanera, bolera* and *danzon* became popular.

The fusion of the above forms of music was marked in the early 1900s by the birth of a new type of music—*son*. A combination of percussion and guitar, son influenced the danzon orchestras and led to the creation of the big-band sound.

In the 1940s and '50s, the *mambo* and the *cha-cha* developed out of the rumba and son. At the same time, jazz (mainly from the U.S.) began to influence Cuban music. Cuban son and other Latin rhythms that were popular in the outskirts of New York combined in the 1960s and '70s to form a loosely defined type of music and dance called *salsa*. The *nueva trova*, which largely consists of political ballads, also came into being during the 1960s and '70s.

Entertainment

From informal music in a cafe or restaurant to the more exotic dancing and singing shows found in many hotels, Cuba never lacks entertainment possibilities. Havana and Santiago de Cuba host world-famous Tropicana cabaret shows, where the style of costume, dance and singing harks back to the 1950s. Discotheques are found in the larger hotels of most cities and cater to a wide range of musical tastes.

Most cities have a casa de trova, which is a club for all types of music. There are also casas de cultura, which are used for more formal performances. It is sometimes possible to see well-known Cuban bands, such as Iraquere and Los Van Van, at informal venues like nightclubs or beer gardens.

A NACHOUM

Cabaret performers offer colorful entertainment.

Festivals & Events

Cuban festivals are lively affairs that combine colorful processions with music and dancing. Originating in colonial times when slaves were given a few days to celebrate the end of the sugar harvest, they act as reminders of Cuba's past. Today, neighborhood religious societies take part in the processions by parading in costumes representative of African folklore and culture.

Cuba's *Carnaval* (Mardi Gras) celebrations, held in Havana, Santiago de Cuba and Varadero, were discontinued after 1990 because of economic hard times, but attempts are underway to revive Havana's Carnaval with outdoor performances on Friday, Saturday and Sunday evenings throughout February. The Jornadas de la Cultura Camagüeyana is scheduled for the first two weeks of February and the Havana International Jazz Festival happens every second year in February. April sees the Semana de la Cultura celebrated in Baracoa and the Electroacoustic Music Festival in Varadero. The first week of May has the Romería de Mayo in Holguín and at the end of June, Trinidad hosts the Fiestas Sanjuaneras. The Festival of Caribbean Culture is celebrated in June or July, October has the 10-day Havana Festival of Contemporary Music, and the Semana de la Cultura Trinitaria happens in Trinidad in late November. The International Festival of Latin-American Film is held in Havana in December of each year.

Labor Day (May 1st) is an important Cuban holiday. On Havana's Plaza de la Revolución, revelers sing patriotic songs and wave banners pertinent to Cuba's revolution. You may even hear Fidel Castro make a speech.

Hiking

The rugged terrain of the Sierra Maestra range dominates the Granma province.

Cuba's lush landscape—dotted with mountains and surrounded by beaches—lends itself well to hiking adventures. Though trail maps are hard to come by and trails themselves may not be well marked, several places are worth a visit.

You can learn about local flora and bird life on the nature trails of **Las Terrazas**, approximately 80km (50 miles) west of Havana. You can also purchase locally made ornaments and works of art. Relatively close to Las Terrazas is **Soroa**, a lush valley famous for its orchids and waterfalls.

In eastern Cuba you'll find the **Gran Parque Nacional Sierra Maestra**, made up of three smaller park areas: **Granma Landing**, **Turquino** and **Gran Piedra**. All provide hiking trails where you're likely to see native birds, reptiles, colorful snails and butterflies. Each area has its own special attraction: Granma Landing is famous for its caves and waterfalls; the highest mountains in Cuba, Pico Turquino and Pico Cuba, can be found in the Turquino area; and Gran Piedra is noted for its 62 endemic species of flora.

The **Baconao Biosphere Reserve** and the protected area of **Pinares de Mayari** are also found in eastern Cuba, between Santiago de Cuba and the Río Baconao. The reserve offers caves, a cactus garden, remains of Spanish forts, a prehistoric valley and 16th-century iron mines. Hiking and bird-watching around Pinares de Mayari take place along a number of marked trails where you'll find pine forests, spectacular mountain views and waterfalls.

Surfing & Windsurfing

The top surfing season is from December to April, when the northeast trade winds are at their strongest and the best breaks are on the Atlantic shores facing north or east. From August to September tropical storms can drive huge waves onto the south coast. Surfers will have to bring their own boards, as they'll find none for rent.

Conditions for windsurfing are often good at Varadero, Guardalavaca, Marea del Portillo and Cayo Largo. Many beach resorts in these areas will rent equipment.

E SNIJDERS

Beachgoers enjoy the warm sun and steady breezes at Guardalavaca beach.

Diving Health & Safety

E SNIDJERS

General Health

Cuba is a relatively low-risk country for foreign travelers concerned about their health and safety. Yellow fever was eliminated in 1901, malaria in 1968 and diphtheria in 1971. Few travelers are likely to experience more than an upset stomach and sunburn. Both can be completely avoided or greatly minimized by following a few simple precautions: Use waterproof sun block and reapply often; drink plenty of liquids and wear a hat when out of the water to help prevent sunburn and heat exhaustion; and limit yourself to "safe" foods like cooked or peeled fruits and vegetables and bottled water or soft drinks.

Pre-Trip Preparation

At least a month before your trip, check your dive gear. Remember, your regulator should be serviced annually, whether you've used it or not. If you use a dive computer and can replace the battery yourself, change it before the trip or buy a spare one to take along. Otherwise, send the computer to the manufacturer for a battery replacement.

If possible, find out if the dive center rents or services the type of gear you own. If not, you might want to take spare parts or even spare gear. A spare mask is always a good idea.

Purchase any additional equipment you might need, such as a dive light and tank marker light for night diving, a line reel for wreck diving, etc. Make sure you have at least a whistle attached to your BC—or even better, add a marker tube (also known as a safety sausage or come-to-me).

Get whatever immunizations you'll need and fill prescriptions. The only immunization currently necessary to enter Cuba is for yellow fever, and then only if you are arriving directly from South America. However, other vaccinations may be worth considering if you plan to travel far off the beaten track. Contact the U.S. Centers for Disease Control for updates via mail, fax or the web. Call (toll-free from the U.S.) ☎ 888-CDC-FAXX and request Document 000005, a list of region-specific publications, available from the CDC. Their website is www.cdc.gov.

About a week before taking off, do a final check of your gear, grease o-rings, check batteries and assemble a save-a-dive kit (and possibly a first aid kit). Don't forget to pack medications such as decongestants, ear drops, antihistamines and seasick tablets.

Tips for Evaluating a Dive Operator

First impressions mean a lot. Does the business appear organized and professionally staffed? Does it prominently display a dive affiliation such as CMAS, ACUC, NAUI, PADI, or SSI? This is a good indication that it adheres to high standards.

When you arrive to dive, a well-run business will always have paperwork for you to fill out. At the least, they should look at your certification card and ask when you last dived.

Rental equipment should be well rinsed. If you see sand or salt crystals, watch out. Before starting on your dive, inspect the equipment thoroughly: Check the hoses for wear, see that mouthpieces are secure and make sure they've given you a depth gauge and air-pressure gauge.

After gearing up and turning on your air, listen for air leaks. Now test your BC: Push the power inflator to make sure it functions correctly (and doesn't free-flow); if it fails, get another BC—don't try to inflate it manually; make sure the BC holds air. Then purge your regulator a bit and smell the air. It should be odorless. If you detect an oily or otherwise bad odor, try a different tank, then start searching for another operator.

E SNIDJERS

DAN

Divers Alert Network (DAN) is an international membership association of individuals and organizations sharing a common interest in diving and safety. It operates a 24-hour diving emergency hot line in the U.S. at ☎ **919-684-8111** or **919-684-4DAN** (-4326). The latter accepts collect calls in a dive emergency. If you have trouble accessing a line to the U.S. from Cuba, try calling DAN Mexico at ☎ **52-5-62-99-800 code 33937** or **4258**, or DAN Europe at ☎ **41-1-383-1111**. DAN does not directly provide medical care; however, it does provide advice on early treatment, evacuation and hyperbaric treatment of diving-related injuries. Divers should contact DAN for assistance as soon as a diving emergency is suspected.

DAN membership is reasonably priced and includes DAN TravelAssist, a membership benefit that covers medical air evacuation from anywhere in the world for any illness or injury. For an additional fee, divers can get secondary insurance coverage for decompression sickness. For membership questions, call ☎ 800-446-2671 in the U.S. or ☎ 919-684-2948 elsewhere.

Medical & Recompression Facilities

On the whole, health services are good for visitors and medical treatment is relatively inexpensive. Hospital emergency departments are open 24 hours a day. Clinics for tourists are available and consultations cost around US$25. Tourists can also get treatment at the *policlínicos* (general hospitals) where Cubans go for minor ailments. Your hotel can usually help you arrange for medical assistance.

H P MAYER-ANHALT
Recompression chamber at
Cárdenas, near Varadero.

Cuba has several recompression chambers. The two main chambers are in Havana and Santiago de Cuba. Smaller hyperbaric units are found in several other areas, including Cárdenas (near Varadero) and Isla de la Juventud.

In the case of an emergency, divers are taken to the nearest chamber by helicopter or other suitable transport. You will need to pay for use of the chamber with cash or credit card before receiving treatment. Claims are later made to your insurance company using the receipt issued by the hyperbaric unit, provided that you were within the limits of your insurance when the accident took place.

Recompression Chambers

The facilities listed below treat dive-related decompression sickness.

Hotel Colony Recompression Chamber
Carretera de la Siguanea, km 41
Colony, Isla de la Juventud
☎ (61) 9-8240 and 9-8282

Gerona Recompression Chamber
Hospital General Docente
Heroes del Baire
Av. 39, Nueva Gerona,
Isla de la Juventud
☎ (61) 2-3012 and 2-4788

Havana Hyperbaric Medical Center
Hospital Naval - Dr. Luis Diaz Soto
Av. Monumental and Carretera del Asilo
Habana del Este, Havana
☎ (7) 97-3266, 62-6825 and
97-4251 through -4256

Hospital Julio Arietegui
Centro de Medicina Subacuática
Carretera de Cárdenas, km 2
Cárdenas, Matanzas
☎ (5) 2-2114

Santiago de Cuba Recompression Chamber
Hospital Militar - Castillo Duany
corner of Punta Blanca and Gasometro
Santiago de Cuba
☎ (226) 2-6471 through -6473

***Ulises* Research Vessel Recompression Chamber**
☎ (7) 61-7643 and 62-1579
Canal 16

Diving in Cuba

Cuba has over 5,700km (3,535 miles) of coastline, with the Atlantic Ocean to the north and the Caribbean Sea to the south. The 12 dive regions described here offer an excellent range of dive sites around the island. Most dives are within an hour's boat ride from a dive base and many can be accessed from shore.

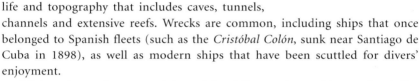

E SNIJDERS

Underwater, you'll find a wide range of marine life and topography that includes caves, tunnels, channels and extensive reefs. Wrecks are common, including ships that once belonged to Spanish fleets (such as the *Cristóbal Colón*, sunk near Santiago de Cuba in 1898), as well as modern ships that have been scuttled for divers' enjoyment.

Diving trips can be arranged through local dive services and international dive package and live-aboard companies (see the "Listings" section for details). Live-aboards, though not common, are particularly convenient for diving the Caribbean

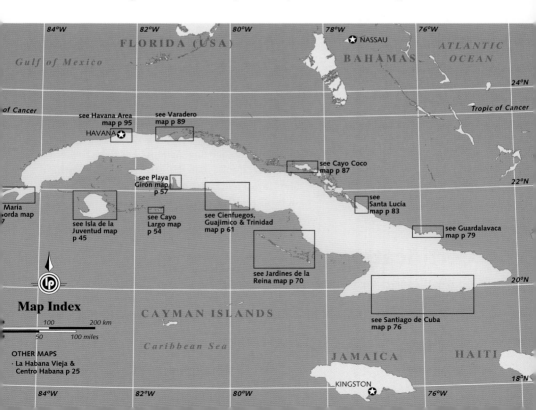

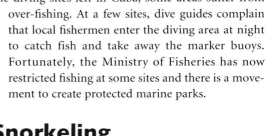

Diving for Treasure

Cuba was a hub for galleon traffic throughout the 17th and 18th centuries. Many of these ships, carrying precious metals, spices and slaves to the New World, were sunk during pirate attacks. Treacherous seas and battles between warring nations also contributed to their demise.

Today, the remains of these vessels occupy the seabed around Cuba. When the ships went under, their treasure often sunk too. CARISUB, a Cuban marine archeological organization, charters tours for the purpose of salvaging the galleons. Scubacan, a Canadian dive tour company, also offers "treasure hunting" tours where participants can dive wrecks alongside Cuban recovery experts. Depending on the location, divers may see relics such as old anchor chains, anchors and cannons. Gold doubloons, however, are much harder to find.

archipelago Jardines de la Reina, where lodging is limited. Most live-aboards and dive packages must be pre-booked.

Though there are pristine diving sites left in Cuba, some areas suffer from over-fishing. At a few sites, dive guides complain that local fishermen enter the diving area at night to catch fish and take away the marker buoys. Fortunately, the Ministry of Fisheries has now restricted fishing at some sites and there is a movement to create protected marine parks.

E SNIJDERS

Cuba's dive sites are rich with marine life.

Snorkeling

On the whole, Cuba has better scuba diving than snorkeling, though regions such as Varadero, Playa Girón and Cienfuegos offer decent snorkeling opportunities. Those with shore access include Punta Perdiz and Playa Coral. Several boat dives shallow enough for snorkelers' enjoyment include: El Arco de los Sabalos, Acuario, Las Rabirruvias, El Bajo, El Naranjo, Bajo de María Aguilar, Aquarium and Cayo Piedras & Cayo Mono. Wreck sites accessible to snorkelers include: *Jibacoa* & *Sparta*, *El Rancho Club* at El Coral and Barco Hundido.

Certification

PADI courses are available in Cayo Largo at the Action Sport Diving Center. CMAS (Confédération Mondiale des Activités Subaquatiques) and ACUC (American Canadian Underwater Certification) courses are available at many other sites. Prices for these courses compare favorably with prices in the rest of the Caribbean.

Specialty courses such as underwater photography and night diving are available at some dive centers, though not all are linked to a diving certification agency. In some cases, joint ventures with foreign companies have been formed, utilizing both Cuban and foreign dive instructors. In general, dive guides exhibit a professional and sensible approach when working with both novice and experienced divers.

Dive Site Icons

The symbols at the beginning of the dive site descriptions provide a quick summary of some of the following characteristics present at the site:

 Good snorkeling or free-diving site.

 Remains or partial remains of a wreck can be seen at this site.

 Sheer wall or drop-off.

 Deep dive. Features of this dive occur in water deeper than 27m (90ft).

 Strong currents may be encountered at this site.

 Strong surge (the horizontal movement of water caused by waves) may be encountered at this site.

 Drift dive. Because of strong currents and/or difficulty in anchoring, a drift dive is recommended at this site.

 Beach/shore dive. This site can be accessed from shore.

 Poor visibility. The site often has visibility of less than 8m (25ft).

 Caves are a prominent feature of this site. Only experienced cave divers should explore inner cave areas.

 Regulations restrict fishing and the removal of marine life in this area.

Free-Diving in Cuba

Cuba is famous not only for its scuba diving, but also for its free-divers. On June 6, 1998 the Cuban Francisco "Pipin" Ferreras set a record when he dived to 156.8m (514.5ft) off Cabo San Lucas, Mexico. He did it by taking a second breath from a half-liter air tank rigged within the depths.

Pipin and his French wife Audrey Mestre set a tandem free-diving record in 1998. The pair dived to 115m (377ft) and remained underwater for 12 minutes and 12 seconds.

Deborah Andollo is another famous Cuban free-diver. At 31 years old, she was the holder of titles in all possible disciplines of depth apnea (free-diving).

Pisces Rating System for Dives & Divers

The dive sites in this book are rated according to the following diver skill-level rating system. These are not absolute ratings but apply to divers at a particular time, diving at a particular place. For instance, someone unfamiliar with prevailing conditions might be considered a novice diver at one dive area, but an intermediate diver at another, more familiar location.

Novice: A novice diver generally fits the following profile:
◆ basic scuba certification from an internationally recognized certifying agency
◆ dives infrequently (less than one trip a year)
◆ logged fewer than 25 total dives
◆ dives no deeper than 18m (60ft)
◆ little or no experience diving in similar waters and conditions
* A novice diver should be accompanied by an instructor, divemaster or advanced diver on all dives

Intermediate: An intermediate diver generally fits the following profile:
◆ may have participated in some form of continuing diver education
◆ logged between 25 and 100 dives
◆ dives no deeper than 40m (130ft)
◆ has been diving within the last six months in similar waters and conditions

Advanced: An advanced diver generally fits the following profile:
◆ advanced certification
◆ has been diving for more than two years and logged over 100 dives
◆ has been diving within the last six months in similar waters and conditions

Regardless of skill level, you should be in good physical condition and know your limitations. If you are uncertain as to your own level of expertise, ask the advice of a local dive instructor. He or she is best qualified to assess your abilities based on the prevailing dive conditions at any given site. Ultimately you must decide if you are capable of making a particular dive, depending on your level of training, recent experience and physical condition, as well as water conditions at the site. Remember that water conditions can change at any time, even during a dive.

María la Gorda Dive Sites

María la Gorda is a remote, beautiful dive region and resort town found 300km (186 miles) west of Havana. The resort's nearby dive sites are on the western tip of the main island in the Bahía de Corrientes, to the south of the Península de Guanahacabibes. The diving here has been described as some of the best in the country. The main dive sites are relatively close to shore—the farthest is reached after a 30-minute boat ride.

Diving is possible year-round because the Bahía de Corrientes is relatively sheltered. Visibility is also good year-round, averaging 16-25m (52-82ft).

María la Gorda is noted for its brightly colored coral formations, sponges and gorgonians. You'll see a profusion of tropicals and perhaps barracuda, moray eels, lobsters or even an occasional whale shark, particularly from late August until November. The remnants of Spanish galleons are also found in these waters.

María la Gorda Dive Sites	Good Snorkeling	Novice	Intermediate	Advanced
1 El Faraón		●		
2 Yemaya				●
3 El Almirante			●	
4 El Salón de María			●	
5 Las Tetas de María		●		
6 Ancla del Pirata		●		
7 Paraíso Perdido			●	

1   El Faraón

A 2m-high giant brown barrel sponge—surrounded by tube, basket and vase sponges—stands on the top of a reef wall at about 22m. The sponge is radiant in the light reflected through the water's surface. When you are positioned below the sponge, in front of the wall, you cannot help but admire its imposing

Location: East side of Bahía de Corrientes

Depth Range: 22m-40m (72-130ft)

Access: Boat

Expertise Rating: Novice

Deep Diving

Several attractions lie at or beyond 40m (130ft), considered the maximum depth limit of sport diving. Before venturing beyond this limit, it is imperative that you understand the risks and develop the skills for deep diving. Classes will teach you how to recognize symptoms of nitrogen narcosis and perform decompression procedures when doing deep or repetitive dives. Know your limits and don't push your luck when it comes to depth.

presence. It is estimated to be more than 100 years old.

There is an abundance of fish life near the sponge, including creole-fish, wrasse, bass, jacks, durgons and chromis.

At 35-40m you will find black coral and many deep-water gorgonians. It is possible to find large lobsters in the wall's crevices. As with the majority of sites at María la Gorda, the coral cover is excellent.

2   Yemaya

In the Santería religion, Yemaya is the elusive "Goddess of the Sea." Perhaps it is the air of mystery attributed to her that inspired this site's name. This Yemaya will not remain a mystery for long, how-

Location: East side of Bahía de Corrientes

Depth Range: 13-32m (42-105ft)

Access: Boat

Expertise Rating: Advanced

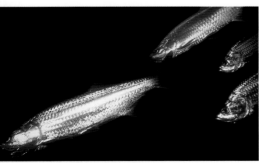
W HARRISON
Tarpon guard the entrance to Yemaya.

ever, as it is only 15 minutes by boat from María la Gorda's dive base.

At 32m you'll enter a small, 2m-high cave that is often guarded by tarpon. From here, you will ascend through a long and gently curving tunnel. A flashlight is required for this dive.

Be Gentle with the Giant

Giant barrel sponges are normally found in quiet water below 12m (40ft). The largest specimens typically occur in deep water along the forward slope of a reef. They can grow to more than 2m (6ft) high with an equal diameter.

Sponges are the simplest of multicellular animals.

Divers are often tempted to enter these large sponges. Handling and entry of barrel sponges is discouraged because the lip breaks easily, disrupting the organism's flow of water and food. Breakage also allows the entry of organisms that can weaken the sponge, which may even cause the colony's death.

Barrel sponges grow only 2cm (1 inch) per year—a sponge large enough for a diver to enter may be more than 100 years old.

Though the tunnel offers little in the way of coral, many divers are attracted to the unique thrill of ascending from 32m to 13m in an enclosed area. This is not advisable for the squeamish or the novice diver: Your buoyancy control must be excellent in order to preserve the tunnel and its life forms. On your journey up you are likely to see small, blind fish.

3 El Almirante

The top of this wall is found at 26m, where you will see huge sponges and gorgonians. Visibility at this site is usually excellent—you can view and photograph the colorful marine life in all its brilliance. Tarpon, angelfish, grunts and groupers populate this area. When you reach 32m, you'll find blooms of black coral.

This wall's backdrop is the beautiful bright-blue water characteristic of María la Gorda dive sites. In areas like this you may be lucky enough to see a whale shark swim by in season.

Location: East side of Bahía de Corrientes

Depth Range: 26-32m (85-105ft)

Access: Boat

Expertise Rating: Intermediate

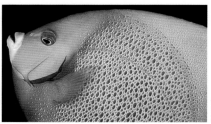

Gray angelfish make great macrophotographic subjects at El Almirante.

The Biggest Fish in the Sea

Human encounters with whale sharks have occurred ever since vessels capable of plying ocean waters were built, but the species was not scientifically described until 1828. Their habit of basking at the surface made them vulnerable to collisions with ships, which were becoming larger and faster. Whale sharks inevitably lost—one giant was even cut completely in half by a steam ship.

The heaviest specimen ever recorded was caught in a fish trap in Siam in 1919. It weighed 41,000kg (90,300lbs) and measured 18m (59ft).

Whale sharks may be found off the coast of Cuba between August and November.

Whale sharks have cartilaginous skeletons, 10cm- (4in-) thick skin and dorsal fins that can grow to 2m (6ft). Though generally found in the open sea, whale sharks are also occasionally seen close to shore. They may be seen off the coast of Cuba between August and November.

4 El Salón de María

El Salón de María is only ten minutes by boat from María la Gorda. This cave, found at 20m, has three entrances. It is characterized by its beautiful furnishings—once inside you will see brightly colored purple, pink, blue and green coral formations and sponges.

Small clusters of sponges and coral form internal pillars in the cave. The trailing whip corals that hang from the ceiling and the abundance of feather stars living within the coral pillars add to this cave's fairy-tale quality.

Look closely at the cave's encrusting sponges, many of which have root-like canals that radiate from the excurrent openings used to release the sponges' food and oxygen. These canals form

Location: East side of Bahía de Corrientes

Depth: 20m (65ft)

Access: Boat

Expertise Rating: Intermediate

attractive patterns, generally star-shaped or flower-like in appearance. In addition to its corals and sponges, the cave is home to basslets, grunts and a few red grouper.

Outside the cave you can see black durgons, snapper, chromis and some large black and Nassau groupers.

5 Las Tetas de María

Las Tetas de María (Maria's Breasts) is found in line with its on-land namesake, a few appropriately shaped rocks that jut out from the shore.

Here you'll find sandy channels weaving around large rocks covered by leaf, brain and lettuce corals. Small and delicate clusters of flower coral, whose branches are tipped with oval cups, can be seen among the larger coral species. Soft corals are plentiful and fish you are likely to see include snappers, angelfish, jacks, groupers and blue chromis.

Large schools of chromis are particularly common at many of the sites around María la Gorda. Though you'll easily notice the bright, electric-blue chromis moving around the reef in large numbers, you'll need to look more closely to see their dowdy relative, the brown chromis.

Location: East side of Bahía de Corrientes

Depth: 25m (82ft)

Access: Boat

Expertise Rating: Novice

Blue chromis and elkhorn coral.

Sandy channels are characteristic of Las Tetas de María.

6 Ancla del Pirata

A 30-minute boat ride from the dive center takes you to the Ancla del Pirata ("Pirate's Anchor"), named after a large anchor found at 15m.

The anchor rests against coral-covered promontories and is covered with crus-

Location: East side of Bahía de Corrientes

Depth: 15m (50ft)

Access: Boat

Expertise Rating: Novice

F ARAZOZA

Ancla del Pirata has many corals, sponges, gorgonians and fish.

taceans, attractive sponges and corals. A prominent group of white feather dusters add to the anchor's beauty.

Behind the promontories lies an attractive and lively wall. Sponges, gorgonians and hard corals are common in this region and you are likely to see snappers, bass, wrasse, jacks, angelfish and squirrelfish. Several arched tunnels provide interesting views of the deep-blue waters that meet the wall.

S SIMONSEN

Squirrelfish feed on invertebrates at night.

7 Paraíso Perdido

At 18m the seabed slopes gently to a drop-off where you'll find delightful coral and fish life. Huge lettuce, plate and flower corals are common and you are likely to see an abundance of sea fans, whips and rods. Be sure not to overlook the large purple basket and green-yellow tube sponges, which make great photo subjects.

As you move closer to the wall, the density of sponges and fans increases. The wall begins at 30m and also supports a great deal of life. Its small holes and crevices offer shelter to invertebrates and a variety of fish. The sea in this region is bright-blue and quite stunning contrasted against the colorful sponges and gorgonians.

Location: East side of Bahía de Corrientes

Depth Range: 18-30m (60-100ft)

Access: Boat

Expertise Rating: Intermediate

You can access shallower spots through sandy channels, which you'll see as you ascend along the wall to the submarine terrace. French and gray angelfish favor these channels, as do grouper, snapper and surgeonfish. Schools of blue chromis add color to this bright and lively scene.

D DOOLEY

Graceful sea fans and colorful sponges make Paraíso Perdido a beautiful dive site.

Isla de la Juventud Dive Sites

Off Cuba's southwest coast is Isla de la Juventud (Isle of Youth), perhaps the country's most famous diving region. Prior to 1978, it was known as Isla de Pinos (Isle of Pines). The name was changed as a tribute to the many students who lived and worked here in the 1960s and 1970s. Diving on the isle has been popular since the 1970s and the region is extremely well-equipped and organized for the sport.

The Isla de la Juventud's peninsula inclines to the northwest and prevailing winds are from east, so the region's dive sites are protected from the Gulf of Mexico's currents and waves. The water in this area is generally calm and visibility is exceptionally good, making it an ideal location for Cuba's annual international underwater-photography competition.

The Diving Center Puerto Sol (based out of the Hotel Colony) offers a range of diving services and has several comfortable boats. There is also a modern on-site recompression chamber, complete

D WILLIAMS

The marina at the Hotel Colony.

Isla de la Juventud Dive Sites

	Good Snorkeling	Novice	Intermediate	Advanced
8 Los Indios Wall			●	
9 Jibacoa & Sparta	●	●		
10 El Arco de los Sábalos	●	●		
11 El Cabezo de las Isabelitas			●	
12 Cueva Azul				●
13 El Escondite del Buzo			●	
14 El Sitio de Todos		●		
15 Pared de Coral Negro			●	
16 El Valle de las Rubias		●		

Ride horses on the beach at the Hotel Colony while you off-gas.

with the services of a dive doctor. From the Colony marina it is possible to reach 56 buoyed dive sites, most within an hour's boat ride from the dive center. Isla de la Juventud dive sites are known for their tunnels, deep canals and underwater valleys. Over 40 varieties of coral can be seen in this area, including elkhorn, staghorn and black coral. You will see large numbers of fish, including small tropicals, tarpon, barracuda, groupers, snooks, grunts and angelfish, and you may encounter sea turtles. East of Punta del Este is an area called Bajo de Zambo, a virtual cemetery of wrecks, where the remains of 70 ships have been found.

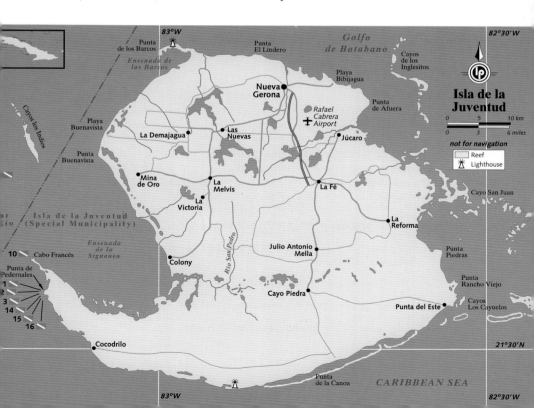

Sea Turtle Conservation

The shell of the hawksbill turtle is made up of overlapping orange, brown and gold scales.

Four turtle species are found in Cuba's waters: leatherback, loggerhead, green and hawksbill. All are endangered or threatened species. The leatherback turtle is the largest, weighing 300-700kg (660-1,540lbs), with a shell length of 108-183cm (42-72 inches). The loggerhead turtle is the second-largest, with a typical weight of 90-160kg (198-352lbs) and a body length of around 1m (3.3ft). The green turtle reaches a length of 1m. The hawksbill is one of the smallest turtles; its shell reaches a maximum length of 90cm (3ft).

Dangers contributing to the demise of these creatures include: hunting for human consumption, turtle-shell jewelry and ornaments; loss of habitat because of tourism and development; pollution; getting trapped in fishing nets; and injury from ship propellers and boat traffic.

To protect these turtles, Cuba has developed a management plan for the Isla de la Juventud and the Archipiélago de los Canarreos areas. The management plan limits the number of turtles that can be captured, prohibits hunting for turtles that are below a certain size and prohibits hunting during the reproductive season. In addition, a turtle-breeding farm (the Experimental Sea Turtle Breeding Center) has been established in the town of Cocodrilo on the Isla de la Juventud. Management plans and breeding efforts are clearly essential for the turtles' survival and effective projects are needed throughout the world to ensure the survival of this special reptile.

What can you do to help turtles survive?

✓ Don't disturb or frighten a sea turtle, especially during mating season (June through August).

✓ Don't eat turtle eggs, turtle soup, or any other turtle dish.

✓ Don't buy or use any product made from turtle shell.

✓ Encourage efforts to preserve turtle-nesting beaches as natural reserves.

8 Los Indios Wall

Just before the wall plummets to the ocean bed, you'll encounter huge rocky turrets covered with lettuce, star and brain corals. Fire coral is also found in this region, so take care not to touch it. Black coral can be seen on the wall at about 30m, along with deep-water gorgonians.

Location: Northwest of Cayos los Indios

Depth Range: 12-30m (40-100ft)

Access: Boat

Expertise Rating: Intermediate

Upon leaving the wall (past the turrets) you will find rocky outcrops covered with coral and plant life standing in the middle of a sandy bed. Fish life around the turrets and along the bed is plentiful.

Divers will often see rays, particularly southern stingrays, in this area. Though these rays normally lie motionless on the sandy bottom, they will make an immediate escape if you come too close to them. The southern stingray can grow up to nearly 2m in diameter and feeds on the small fish and invertebrates that it uncovers by making indentations in the sand.

Southern stingrays can grow to nearly 2m.

9 Jibacoa & Sparta

This site offers not just one wreck, but two: the *Jibacoa*, once a cargo ship, and the *Sparta*, a military ship. Both ships were originally used for military target practice and were intentionally sunk in the late 1970s. Since that time, marine life has established itself in and around the wrecks and the site has become a favorite haunt for divers and snorkelers.

Location: Southwest of Cayos los Indios

Depth Range: 0-8m (0-26ft)

Access: Boat

Expertise Rating: Novice

The *Jibacoa* is partly out of the water and visible from the surface, while the *Sparta*, complete with guns, is found lying on its side.

Although the openings and the doors are sufficiently wide for a safe entry, excellent buoyancy control is required to avoid damaging the corals and encrusting sponges. Both wrecks are breeding grounds for many species of fish, thus a special importance is placed on protecting the site.

Schools of snapper are a common sight here—you'll see them moving through and around the more exposed parts of the wrecks. Their bland coloring contrasts well with the sometimes vivid colors of the corals, algae and sponges growing on the wreck.

This site is made even more beautiful by its colorful tropicals, including gobies, blennies and wrasse, which you'll find as you explore the wrecks' recesses. You can also see small crabs and urchins hiding in holes and are likely to see a number of inquisitive barracuda as you look away from the wrecks.

There are many photo opportunities on, in and around these wrecks—fish and fixtures such as anchor ropes, guns and ladders encrusted with colorful

Wreck Diving

Wreck diving can be safe and fascinating. Penetration of shipwrecks, however, is a skilled specialty and should not be attempted without proper training. Wrecks are often unstable and they can be silty, deep and disorienting. Use an experienced guide to view wrecks and the amazing coral communities that have developed on them.

coral make good photo subjects. The shallow depth allows for a lot of light, which gives greater brilliance to the marine life found on the ships' exteriors.

Both the *Jibacoa* and the *Sparta* wrecks offer unique photo opportunities.

10 El Arco de los Sábalos

This dive site's name, translated as "The Arch of the Tarpon," is an accurate description of what you will find here. A rocky coral-covered arch stands high in the midst of a colorful and lively coral garden. You'll find tarpon weaving their way in and around the arch. The seabed here is relatively flat, with the arch serving as the focal point of the open area.

Corals and sponges in this area are colorful and you are sure to see many friendly yellowtail snappers, common in Cuba's waters. These fish, with their brilliant yellow midbody stripe and tail, are unafraid and often closely approach divers. Full-grown yellowtail measure up to 65cm (25 inches) and feed at night on crustaceans and small fish. Juvenile yellowtail feed on plankton.

Location: Northwest of Cabo Francés

Depth: 13m (43ft)

Access: Boat

Expertise Rating: Novice

U NATOLI
Yellowtail are curious and often follow divers.

11 El Cabezo de las Isabelitas

El Cabezo is an exceptionally photogenic site because of the good visibility and natural light available at this depth, and because of its diversity of marine life. Move directly down from the marker buoy to reach a large number of coral outcrops surrounded by sand. Star, lettuce and brain corals are common. Above the coral heads you will see a multitude of small reef fish.

As you approach the wall, the topography becomes more rugged and the marine life becomes more dense. Snappers, goatfish, parrotfish, hamlets, angelfish, trumpetfish and the occasional barracuda are seen here. You can also see squirrelfish hiding in the

Location: West of Punta de Pedernales

Depth: 15m (50ft)

Access: Boat

Expertise Rating: Novice

nooks and crannies. Among the corals are green-tipped anemones and various sponges, including tubes and vases.

The small sandy channels make this dive memorable—they slope sharply to the edge of the wall, searing their way through the lively, bright coral formations.

12 Cueva Azul

When you dive El Sitio de Todos, you hover above the tarpon—on this dive you enter their realm. Divers descend single file through a 3-5m-wide vertical chimney that runs from the top of the wall (at about 14m) to 42m. At the top of the wall and en route down the gully you will pass through schools of tarpon, many of which grow to nearly 2m. Though the

Location: West of Punta de Pedernales

Depth Range: 14-42m (45-137ft)

Access: Boat

Expertise Rating: Advanced

W HARRISON

Diver investigates hole at the base of Cueva Azul.

wall drops for nearly 1000m, the deepest point of this dive is marked by the 2.5m-wide hole you'll find at 42m. In and around it are many sparkling silversides.

From the hole, swim along the wall for about 100m. From this point, divers either ascend though a second gully or up the face of the wall. The contrasting blues are spectacular, changing as you progress through the dive. You'll see various species of gorgonians as you ascend; however, it is not until you reach the wall's plateau that you'll fully experience the prolific marine life of the site: large rays, sharks, barracuda, very large angelfish and a wide variety of colorful sponges.

13 El Escondite del Buzo

This site offers two exciting dive possibilities: Either meander through the beautiful coral gardens at approximately 15m or use these gardens to access a deeper dive that is along a wall at 30m. This deeper dive is more suitable for intermediate or advanced divers.

Whether you undertake the shallower or the deeper dive, most divers move south along the line of the dropoff. In the shallower region there are a number of gullies where you will see a variety of fish, corals and smaller invertebrates.

Location: West of Punta de Pedernales

Depth Range: 15-30m (50-100ft)

Access: Boat

Expertise Rating: Intermediate

Southern stingrays, groupers, gray snappers and jewfish in particular are found in this area. Schools of jacks and blue chromis are a common sight, and various gobies are found close to the coral heads. Feather dusters and Christmas tree worms are common invertebrates. You'll see star, brain and whip corals interspersed with sea fans. Closer to and on the wall you'll find many sponges. Yellow and green tube sponges are particular to this area, as are small vase sponges.

14 El Sitio de Todos

This is a lively and colorful reef with many tropicals weaving their way around sea fans, small crops of hard coral and bright sponges. Upon closer inspection you will find anemones, a wide variety of marine invertebrates, crabs and snails.

Location: West of Punta de Pedernales

Depth: 15m (50ft)

Access: Boat

Expertise Rating: Novice

Start by heading west: Before you reach the reef's edge you will cross some deep, jagged, vertical gullies, common to many of the dive sites in this area. One of these gullies marks the way to Cueva Azul.

This dive is normally undertaken after a deeper dive on the outer wall. It is a good place to take pictures, especially for novice photographers, because the area receives a lot of light and the fish are relatively tame. Tarpon, in particular, show no fear when confronted with inquisitive divers. You are likely to see many types of fish, such as yellowtail snappers, butterflyfish, parrotfish, gobies and jacks.

Colorful marine life and excellent visibility attract photographers to Isla de la Juventud's reefs.

A NACHOUM

15 Pared de Coral Negro

As the name suggests, this site is famous for its black coral, found along the wall at 35m. Farther up the wall are bright sponges and corals, including elkhorn, staghorn and brain corals. Yellow and green tube sponges are common, as are small basket sponges. The fish that inhabit these waters include tarpon, snappers, hamlets and parrotfish.

Location: West of Punta de Pedernales

Depth: 35m (114ft)

Access: Boat

Expertise Rating: Intermediate

On reaching the reef front, the fish life becomes more prolific. Yellowtail snapper is abundant, and you may see queen parrotfish, hogfish, both gray and French angelfish and schoolmasters.

You are likely to find green moray eels hiding in the rock's holes and crevices during the day. The green moray, which can grow to more than 2m, is the largest of the morays found in the Atlantic/Caribbean region. Its fluorescent green color is attributed to a yellowish mucus that overlays its dark blue skin.

Moray eels, often found in holes and crevices, are usually wary of divers.

Black Coral Structure

Black coral polyps secrete a protein laid down in concentric layers forming branched or wire-like skeletons. The cross section of these branches looks like the growth rings of a tree. Though the protein is usually black, most black corals take on a hint of color (gray, brown, rust-red or green) from the polyps that live on the skeletal surface. Each polyp has six small nonretractable tentacles that are normally visible to the naked eye. The form and spacing of these polyps make black coral easy to distinguish from other species: They are spaced apart from one another and their tentacle clusters look like barbed wire. Polyps of other species are often closely spaced and difficult to distinguish as individual tentacles.

Because of the commercial value of black coral, many species are now rare from overharvesting. Visitors to Cuba can discourage the harvesting of ever-diminishing stocks of black coral by not purchasing black-coral jewelry and souvenirs.

16 El Valle de las Rubias

Here you'll find small, sandy canals weaving their way through coral-covered rock formations. You'll see soft corals, lettuce corals, star corals and gorgonians, which are common to many of the sites in this region.

What makes this site so special is the large number of fish species. Nassau

Location: West of Punta de Pedernales

Depth: 12m (40ft)

Access: Boat

Expertise Rating: Novice

Beware of well-camouflaged scorpionfish.

groupers inhabit the area, along with black durgons, barracuda and smaller tropicals. When you look in the nooks and crannies you are likely to find crabs and moray eels.

You may see spotted scorpionfish camouflaged close to the rocks. Be careful not to touch them as they have venomous foredorsal fins that, when raised defensively, can inflict a painful wound.

Cayo Largo Dive Sites

Cayo Largo is the largest island in the Archipiélago de los Canarreos, which lies east of Isla de la Juventud. The archipelago is made up of many small cayes with white sandy beaches. Live-aboards frequently visit this area.

Cayo Largo has around 30 dive sites. The three described below are in the Arrecifes los Ballenatos. Nearby are two other diving areas. The area near Cayo Rosario, just 30km (19 miles) west, offers an underwater landscape of coral mounts. The waters close to Cayo Sigua and Cayos Blancos, about 48km (30 miles) northeast, are noted for their variety of sponges, gorgonians and black coral.

D WILLIAMS
Thatched umbrellas, Cayo Largo beach.

Cayo Largo is known for its shallow-water coral gardens. The sea here is very clear and its reefs offer spectacular diving opportunities. Drop-offs begin at around 6m (20ft), with some reaching tremendous depths. In deeper water you'll find steep and craggy walls with an abundance of marine life: invertebrates, jacks, tarpon and colorful tropicals. Within the area you are likely to see green and hawksbill turtles, along with sharks and many lobsters.

Cayo Largo Dive Sites

	Good Snorkeling	Novice	Intermediate	Advanced
17 Acuario	●	●		
18 Las Rabirruvias	●	●		
19 Cuevas del Negro			●	

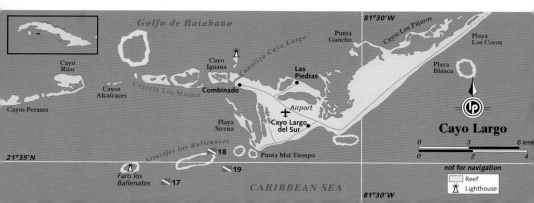

17 Acuario

It is quite easy to see why this area is named "Aquarium." The variety of species here is phenomenal. Clouds of snappers (including schoolmaster, yellowtail snappers and lane snappers) as well as jacks and wrasse can be found all over the patch reefs that characterize this site.

The giant crabs, eels (including spotted eels), spiders, Christmas tree worms and other invertebrates living in the small holes and caves found throughout the area provide many macrophotographic opportunities. You will also see

Location: Southeast of the lighthouse Los Ballenatos

Depth Range: 12-15m (40-50ft)

Access: Boat

Expertise Rating: Novice

squirrelfish, soldierfish, scorpionfish, porcupinefish and even spotted drums. Cornetfish are common, as are trumpetfish, butterflyfish and rock beauties.

G CIOTERA

A variety of fish congregate over Acuario's patch reefs.

18 Las Rabirruvias

Small coral outcrops thrive in the middle of bright white sand. Soft corals and purple sea fans wave in the gentle current. Large parrotfish, hogfish, angelfish, yellowtail and other types of snapper are found around the outcrops. Look closely at the sand to find well-camouflaged flounder. There is also a vast array of conches in this area.

Location: Southwest of Playa la Sirena

Depth Range: 5-8m (16-26ft)

Access: Boat

Expertise Rating: Novice

Attractive coral outcrop at Las Rabirruvias.

Away from the main centers of activity you may see barracuda and even some rays. You can find moray eels, soldierfish and squirrelfish hiding in the small crevices and holes of the outcrops. This site is flanked by a larger reef which has sizable coral formations, including elkhorn and brain coral.

Las Rabirruvias is also an excellent night dive, as many of the creatures that live here come out to feed at night and stay hidden during the day.

19 Cuevas del Negro

At 25m you'll have an excellent view of Cuevas del Negro. As you look down you'll see a large, sandy valley that twists its way around the base of a sharp and imposing ridge. Large tarpon gather here in the darkness of their own silent valley. At 30m there are small, dark recesses in the canyon where you'll find more tarpon and even some sea bass.

Nearby are huge plate-coral formations. Black coral is also found in this region at around 40m. Along the ledge

Location: Southwest of Punta Mal Tiempo

Depth Range: 25-35m (82-115ft)

Access: Boat

Expertise Rating: Intermediate

and in shallower depths you will see porcupinefish, angelfish and jacks.

Playa Girón Dive Sites

Cuba's south shore holds many delights for the diver. Northeast of Cayo Largo on the Cuban mainland is Playa Girón. This beach, which lies east of the mouth of Bahía de Cochinos (also known as the Bay of Pigs) gained notoriety as the site of the unsuccessful April 14, 1961 attack led by CIA-trained Cuban émigrés.

Many divers are surprised to learn that there is good diving in the infamous Bay of Pigs. The bay is accessed from the village of Playa Larga, 115km (71 miles) southeast of Havana, and is a good option for a day trip when northern dive sites near Havana have poor weather or water conditions. The dive centers in Playa Larga and Playa Girón have their own compressors and a range of rental equipment.

Diving here is excellent, characterized by abrupt drop-offs close to shore, swim-throughs and plentiful gorgonians, corals and sponges. Groupers and barracuda are often seen. You can also explore the wreck of a ship scuttled in 1994. Two boats from the 1961 invasion are in the bay but are inaccessible to divers due to their depth and distance from shore.

This region also has some easy-access, shallow shore dives where both divers and snorkelers are likely to see colorful patch reefs and many species of fish, including parrotfish, jackknife fish, damsels, butterflyfish, creole-fish, cardinalfish, blennies, gobies and jawfish. Nearby there are inland cave dives at El Brinco and La Cueva de las Peces, northwest of the city of Playa Girón.

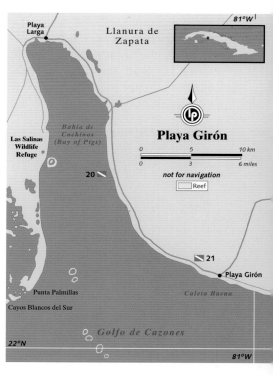

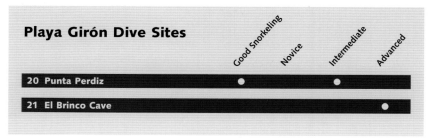

Playa Girón Dive Sites

Playa Girón Dive Sites	Good Snorkeling	Novice	Intermediate	Advanced
20 Punta Perdiz		●	●	
21 El Brinco Cave				●

20 Punta Perdiz

Punta Perdiz is one of Playa Girón's best shore dives. A few metal steps provide access to the beach and water. To get to Punta Perdiz divers normally swim west out to sea for about ten minutes over colorful patch reefs.

Soon you will find a fantastic wall at around 18m. The sponge life on this wall is incredible. As you move southeast along the wall at about 30m, you will see huge twisting rope, tube, vase, barrel, encrusting and even elephant ear sponges. There are also many corals, including disc and plate corals. Fish life along the wall includes snappers, angelfish, trumpetfish and perhaps even a barracuda or two.

Location: East coast of Bahía de Cochinos

Depth Range: 6-30m (20-100ft)

Access: Shore

Expertise Rating: Intermediate

Returning to your initial entry point, you'll pass over colorful patch reefs that are good for snorkeling. In this area you are likely to see more fish including parrotfish, jackknife fish, damsels, butterflyfish, creole-fish, cardinalfish, blennies, gobies and jawfish.

Sponge and coral landscape of Playa Girón.

21　El Brinco Cave

El Brinco is an unusual and special inland cave dive. Because of the risks associated with cave diving, you should only dive this site with a qualified guide. To get there from Playa Girón, drive 2km northwest along the coast (on the road heading to the Autopista). On the right is a small and overgrown turnoff. Continue on this turnoff for about five minutes, then make another right turn. You will soon arrive at El Brinco Cave. It is best to plan your dive at El Brinco for around noon—you will benefit from the natural light entering the cave at that time.

At first sight the cave does not appear particularly welcoming. It is small and dark, and its appearance is not helped by the leaves floating on the water's surface. It is what lies below the surface that lures divers here.

Be careful descending the slippery concrete steps into the cave. Though metal steps permit entry into the cave's waters, they are very steep and are probably better for making an exit. To enter, throw your inflated BC and tank into the water first, then jump in and put your equipment on with the help of your buddy. This is especially appropriate when you know the meaning of the dive site name: El Brinco means "The Jump."

Once in the cave's water, a mix of saltwater and freshwater, the usual profile for this dive is to head east down to 38m. A thin line marks this route. At the end of the cave you'll find a large rock from which there is an easily accessible short tunnel. Following the tunnel up, you'll once again exit into the main pool at 34m.

Location: 2km (1.5miles) northwest of Playa Girón

Depth Range: 34-38m (111-125ft)

Access: Road

Expertise Rating: Advanced

Unlike the inland Saturno Caves near Varadero, El Brinco has no stalactites or stalagmites. Blind fish inhabit the cave and you might find old shells in the rock.

At around noon a shaft of light penetrates the cave's roof and reaches straight down through the water to 42m. The shaft widens as the sun moves higher in the sky.

It is not necessary to go to the cave's bottom to get the full effect of this light. Position yourself at a comfortable depth out of the light shaft to observe this beautiful sight. The light's bright, golden color contrasts impressively with the water's green hue.

Inland Cave Diving

Inland cave diving, also known as cenote (si-**no**-tee) diving, can be a wonderful entrance into the underground world of stalactites, stalagmites, blind fish and other phenomena. It is important to receive proper training in order to safely enjoy this unique underwater world. The risk of becoming disoriented or lost and running out of air make cave diving a dangerous activity. It should be undertaken only by advanced divers trained in cave diving and led by a guide who is familiar with the cave.

Cienfuegos, Guajimico & Trinidad Dive Sites

Along the central southern shore are the diving areas of Cienfuegos, Guajimico and Trinidad. Though they share much of the marine life common to this region, there are topographical elements that are unique to each underwater environment.

The resort at Guajimico offers attractive beaches at the foot of the Escambray mountains.

Cienfuegos, Guajimico & Trinidad Dive Sites	Good Snorkeling	Novice	Intermediate	Advanced
22 La Corona			●	
23 El Coral	●	●		
24 El Laberinto			●	
25 *Camaronero 2*		●		
26 El Bajo	●	●		
27 El Naranjo	●	●		
28 La Punta Arriba			●	
29 Blue Canyon			●	
30 Bajo de María Aguilar	●	●		
31 Cayo Blanco Area				●

Cienfuegos Area

This dive area is a 20-minute drive from the revolutionary city of Cienfuegos, one of the first cities to be taken by Castro and his *compadres*. Just east of the mouth of Bahía de Cienfuegos are several dive sites notable for their coral gardens and proliferation of sponges. The area's deep channels and shipwrecks provide the perfect environment for a plethora of marine creatures.

Most dive sites can be reached within 30 minutes by boat from the local dive centers. The hotels Rancho Luna and Faro de Luna offer a range of dive services.

E SNIJDERS

Cienfuegos is known for its prolific coral gardens.

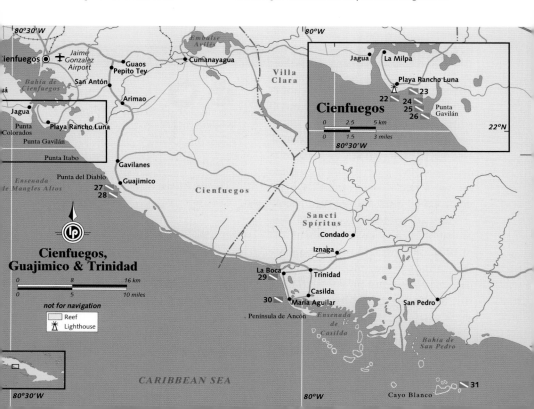

22 La Corona

The best parts of this wall dive are found between 15m and 35m. A variety of corals thrive here, including star, sheet and small blooms of black coral. Several species of sponges (basket and tube sponges, in particular) are also commonly found.

Location: South of the lighthouse

Depth Range: 15-35m (50-115 ft)

Access: Boat

Expertise Rating: Intermediate

Perhaps what makes this dive so special is its larger marine life. It is not unusual to see barracuda, nurse sharks, tarpon, large snappers and ocean trig- gerfish. You may even see whale sharks from August to November.

Nurse sharks are generally harmless but may bite if provoked.

G GOTERA/CUBANACÁN

23 El Coral

This site is named for the immense tower of pillar coral that stands tall in front of a lively reef. Elkhorn, brain, star, lettuce and soft corals also populate the area. You are likely to see sea urchins, crabs and many other invertebrates tucked into the reef's nooks and crannies. On the sandy seabed you'll find sea cucumbers.

Location: East of the lighthouse

Depth Range: 8-14m (26-50ft)

Access: Boat

Expertise Rating: Novice

The scattered remains of an old ship, probably a fishing boat, rest about a 5- to 10-minute swim southeast from the reef. Although not much marine life has set up residence on the wreck, it is still interesting to try to identify the ship's parts.

On this same dive you can visit another wreck, the passenger ship *Rancho* *Club,* which you will find a short distance east of the first. The wreck was nearly intact until 1996 when Hurricane Lili struck. Though its remains litter the seabed now, it is still worth a visit. Several species of tropical fish inhabit the area, and sponges and soft corals live on this ship's scattered pieces.

24 El Laberinto

On this dive you'll weave your way through a labyrinth of small, sandy gullies surrounded by large coral-covered promontories. There are many routes for divers to follow. Because it is easy to become disoriented in this maze, it is best to let a dive guide lead the way.

In the labyrinth, you'll see a variety of coral, including brain, lettuce, plate and mustard hill corals. The sponge cover is quite varied.

On the edge of the labyrinth at about 27m, you will find a ridge on which you can see small blooms of black coral and plenty of sea rods and fingers. After ascending the ridge, you'll reach a lively coral garden close to the labyrinth, which is a good place to end the dive. Here, a profusion of life awaits you. Large groups of blue tangs, chromis, snappers and groupers favor this area. Upon close inspection you may see moray eels, crabs, feather dusters and Christmas tree worms residing in the coral, which includes star and soft corals. There are also a great number of sea fans.

Location: East of the lighthouse

Depth Range: 12-27m (40-88ft)

Access: Boat

Expertise Rating: Intermediate

Throughout Cienfuegos, you'll see many attractive and pristine corals like this sea fan.

25 *Camaronero 2*

Camaronero 2 was a fishing boat intentionally scuttled in the 1970s. Given the relatively brief period that it has been underwater, a great deal of marine life has taken hold. As you move around the upright hull, you'll see encrusting sponges, disc and pencil corals, algae and different types of hydroids and worms. Together they create an extremely colorful picture.

On the ship's deck there are some medium-sized purple tube sponges and throughout the ship you can find trailing white hydroids. *Camaronero 2* is a good

Location: Northwest of Punta Gavilán

Depth Range: 16-22m (52-72ft)

Access: Boat

Expertise Rating: Novice

place to view colorful tropicals including blue tangs, wrasse and butterflyfish.

Though the wreck is small, it can be safely penetrated. Inside, you'll see attractive orange encrusting sponges. Take care not do disrupt or damage the marine life while exploring the ship.

Inside the wreck, divers' bubbles exit through the ship's funnel. Position yourself outside of the ship to watch this strange phenomenon, which becomes even more remarkable when divers deliberately release air directly under the funnel. It's almost as if *Camaronero 2* has decided to sail again, with the air bubbles looking like smoke from the ship's engines.

You will see a variety of coral, including plate, leaf, flower, whip and mustard hill corals on the imposing pinnacles that lie close to the wreck. There are also a few small canyons with sandy bottoms overhung by plate coral and rope sponges. The top of the coral pinnacles is found at 16m, with the bottom of the canyons found at 20-22m. Around this area you are likely to see a variety of fish including angelfish, damselfish, porgies, rock beauties, grunts, snappers and parrotfish (particularly stoplight parrotfish).

26 El Bajo

El Bajo is characterized by a beautiful and lively reef top. Moray and spotted eels are common here, and it is also possible to see rays and lobsters. Hard corals and sponges are plentiful, as are gorgonians.

This site makes a superb night dive. Squirrelfish, cardinalfish and some corals feed at night, so you will be

Location: West of Punta Gavilán

Depth Range: 4-9m (13-30ft)

Access: Boat

Expertise Rating: Novice

Parrotfish are primary contributors of sand to reefs.

presented with a lively and colorful scene.

Look into crevices to find sleeping parrotfish, which protect themselves at night by covering themselves with a mucus cocoon. It is thought that the cocoon serves to inhibit their predators' ability to smell them.

Parrotfish are active daytime feeders, eating algae that grows on coral and rock. The coral and rock are ground and eaten along with the algae and expelled after they have done their job as a digestive aid. This makes parrotfish one of the most important producers of sand and sediment on the coral reef.

Guajimico & Trinidad Area

Guajimico is an attractive, small resort and dive area nestled at the foot of the Escambray mountains, 40km (25 miles) from Cienfuegos. The majority of Guajimico's dive sites are close to the dive base, on average 20 minutes by boat. Visibility is generally excellent. Its colorful coral gardens are inhabited by a wide variety of tropical fish.

Trinidad, which is about 45km (27 miles) southeast of Guajimico, is a colonial town that was declared a National Heritage Site by UNESCO in 1988. It has three diving areas: Cayo Blanco, Ensenada de Casilda and part of the

Península de Ancón. Cayo Blanco is farthest away from the dive center, approximately an hour and a half by boat. Most of the other sites are much closer. Plentiful coral and tropical fish life are found at each of these areas. Yellowtail and cubera snappers, angelfish, gobies, bass, wrasse, jacks and damselfish live in these waters. Occasionally you may even see turtles.

D WILLIAMS

Enjoy a peaceful stroll along Trinidad's historic streets.

27 El Naranjo

Like a colorful aquarium, El Naranjo is home to a wide variety of fish and coral species. This is a shallow dive, with most of your time spent at 5-6m. Divers usually begin by heading west, then continue on a circular, counter-clockwise route to the east.

On your circuit you are likely to encounter lettuce and fire corals, as well as many gorgonians. There are also anemones. Cubera, dog, lane and yellowtail snappers are a few fish you will likely see, as well as blue damselfish

Location: Southwest of Guajimico

Depth Range: 5-6m (17-20ft)

Access: Boat

Expertise Rating: Novice

and gray and French angelfish. This is also a good site to search for small invertebrates, particularly snails and feather stars.

Living Fossils

Feather stars (also called crinoids) are the most ancient of living echinoderms. They may be found in narrow crevices with only their arms visible, or high atop coral heads. They have small, flat pentagonal bodies with five arms that fork one or more times. Multiple short appendages extend along both sides of each arm, like the quill and vanes of a feather. These pinnate arms are used to filter water for particles of food.

Most feather stars hide their bodies in a recess, exposing only their arms.

Several species of feather stars are abundant to common throughout the Caribbean, including the golden crinoid (both black with yellow-tip and greenish varieties) and the swimming crinoid.

28 La Punta Arriba

After passing through some coral outcrops separated by sand, you will reach the wall at La Punta Arriba. An incredible diversity of coral (including lettuce corals, star corals and different types of soft coral) grows along this wall at an average depth of 30m. Framed against the stunning bright-blue backdrop of the Caribbean, these corals make exceptional photography subjects.

Location: Southwest of Guajimico

Depth: 30m (98ft)

Access: Boat

Expertise Rating: Intermediate

Yellow tube sponges and encrusting sponges in blue, pink, orange and lilac are common, adding further color to this scene.

The fish you are likely to see at this site include schools of chromis, blue damselfish and possibly barracuda. You may also find lobsters resting in the recesses near the top of the wall.

A lobster rests among attractive corals and sponges.

29 Blue Canyon

Begin this dive by heading through some patch reefs, which become more dense as you approach a dramatic wall at around 20m. While descending along the wall to 25-30m and heading north, you will see many coral species. Large plate corals are particularly prominent, as well as disc, brain and star corals. You will also see large yellow tube, rope and reddish encrusting sponges. It's a good place to take wide-angle shots of the colorful and dramatic drop-off against the blue sea.

Location: West of Trinidad

Depth Range: 20-30m (66-98ft)

Access: Boat

Expertise Rating: Intermediate

blue chromis. If you look closely, you can also spot flamingo tongue snails.

Though there are smaller channels in this area, exit the wall via a large sandy channel or canyon. One of the larger canyons (named Blue Canyon) is overhung by whip corals and rope sponges. Fish species you'll see in the canyon include damselfish, a few gray snappers, grunts, squirrelfish and rock hinds.

On your return to the top of the wall, you'll see many small tropicals among the venus sea fans and sea rods, including gobies, yellowhead and bluehead wrasse and schools of

J WEBBER

On top of the wall you will see many sea fans and sea rods.

30 Bajo de María Aguilar

This dive, which takes place in relatively shallow water, is good for both the novice diver and the snorkeler. The underwater terrain consists of small, colorful patch reefs surrounded by white sand. As is typical of the waters around Trinidad, there are many pristine corals, including a mountain of pillar coral.

On and around the corals you are likely to see many worms, encrusting sponges, squirrelfish and basslets. Lobsters

Location: West of Casilda

Depth: 8m (26 ft)

Access: Boat

Expertise Rating: Novice

and banded coral shrimp are often found living in the nooks and crannies.

Banded coral shrimp normally retreat into a protective recess when approached, but the patient diver may be rewarded: If you extend your bare hand to this species of shrimp, it may leave its sanctuary and "clean" your fingers.

M LAWRENCE

Banded coral shrimp remove parasites and bacterial debris from fish.

31 Cayo Blanco Area

The Cayo Blanco Area is less a specific dive site than a general region with similar characteristics throughout. The area lies along reefs off the southeast coast of Bahía de San Pedro. Because the currents can sometimes be strong in this area, time your dives carefully. Local dive operators will know when it is safest and most rewarding to dive. Visibility is generally better here during the winter.

Location: Southeast of Bahía de San Pedro

Depth Range: 12-35m (40-115ft)

Access: Boat

Expertise Rating: Advanced

Around the Cayo Blanco Area you have three distinct diving opportunities: on a reef at 12-15m; along a wall (normally at a depth of 25m); or at about 35m, where colonies of black coral can be found. All areas are good for spotting larger fish, including tarpon, jewfish, barracuda and different species of rays.

Jardines de la Reina Dive Sites

The Archipiélago de los Jardines de la Reina lies 80km (50 miles) south of the main island of Cuba. It is a 160km- (100 mile-) long chain of low coral cayes. Mangroves cover much of these cayes and the beaches are generally small. The small town of Júcaro is the mainland's jumping-off point for the dive sites, and is just two hours by road east of Trinidad.

The only permanent lodging available in the archipelago is the floating hotel called La Tortuga Lodge. This converted barge provides comfortable live-aboard-style accommodations and caters mainly to divers. Live-aboard boats frequently visit this region as well.

These "Gardens of the Queen" attract a great deal of interest among international divers for many reasons. The region has mild current conditions and excellent visibility. There are many pristine corals and the marine landscape includes spectacular walls, wide plateaus and deep channels. Here you can see sharks (particularly silky, blacktip and bull sharks) and quantities of fish including groupers, crevalle jacks, tarpon and bonefish. The best time to see whale sharks in this region is in November and early December.

The floating La Tortuga Lodge is a convenient base for Jardines de la Reina divers to stay.

Jardines de la Reina Dive Sites	Good Snorkeling	Novice	Intermediate	Advanced
32 Farallón			●	
33 Pipin			●	
34 Avalon				●
35 Meseta de los Meros			●	
36 Faisy		●		
37 La Cueva del Pulpo			●	
38 Cabezo de Coral Negro				●

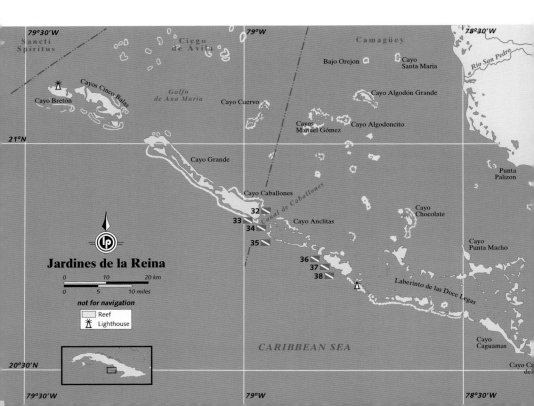

32 Farallón

The underwater terrain at Farallón consists of five tall coral pinnacles: The top of the tallest is at 20m. The pinnacles are separated by small sandy channels at 28m. Meander through the channels, which are overhung by rope sponges, whip corals and gorgonians growing

Location: East of Cayo Caballones

Depth Range: 20-28m (65-92ft)

Access: Boat

Expertise Rating: Intermediate

Tarpon like to inhabit sheltered areas.

from the pinnacle walls. In the more sheltered areas you'll see tarpon and some small tropicals.

While passing through the channels and ascending back to the buoy you will see many pristine corals: small clusters of flower coral living among plate corals, cactus corals, saucer corals and many varieties of soft coral. The fish species that you are likely to encounter include jewfish and other groupers, queen triggerfish, barracuda and crevalle jacks. This is a good area to spot silky sharks and possibly even eagle rays.

33 Pipin

At this site you'll find a platform at around 15m that slopes gently down to 22m, where the wall begins. The coral life on the platform and on the slope is profuse. Plate, star and brain corals abound.

The platform also has a number of sandy surge channels and gullies. In the gullies you can see large shining tarpon weaving their way around each other. Other species you are likely to encounter on this dive include snappers, groupers, jacks, filefish, silky sharks and turtles.

Trunkfish are also common here. This member of the boxfish family looks similar to the cowfish, which is distinguished

Location: South of Cayo Caballones

Depth Range: 15-22m (50-72ft)

Access: Boat

Expertise Rating: Intermediate

by a sharp spine over each eye. Boxfish are protected by enlarged, thickened and sutured scale plates that cover most of their body. They have small protruding mouths and fan-like tails, and propel themselves with their dorsal, anal and pectoral fins.

34 Avalon

Move east from the fixed buoy over coral pinnacles to reach a flat sandy area at 37m. This is a good spot to look for black-tip and silky sharks, which often inhabit this area.

Though curious, blacktip sharks tend to keep their distance. You can identify them by the black markings on the tips of the pectoral, dorsal and lower lobe of the tail fin and by the subtle white band that runs along the side of the body.

The silky shark, on the other hand, has a smooth "silky" skin and is black to gray in color with a whitish tone underneath. The silky shark also has a thin interdorsal ridge on the back. The sharks' movements are rapid and dart-

Location: West of Cayo Anclitas

Depth: 37m (121ft)

Access: Boat

Expertise Rating: Advanced

ing, so if you want to photograph them you will have to be prepared.

In the same area you are likely to see different types of groupers, plenty of yellowtail and gray snapper, crevalle jacks and some barracuda—though many would argue that the highlight of this dive is the sharks.

35 Meseta de los Meros

Meseta de los Meros is about 20 minutes by boat from the floating hotel La Tortuga. Here the seabed juts out in the form of a small rounded table at a depth of 32m, beyond which a wall plummets to infinite depths.

Meseta has some good coral cover including plate, finger and elliptical star

Location: Southwest of Cayo Anclitas

Depth: 32m (105ft)

Access: Boat

Expertise Rating: Intermediate

coral, as well as the usual abundance of gorgonians found in Cuba's waters. There are also many brown-colored tube and basket sponges.

Though the corals are good at this site, it is the fish life above the coral heads that is the main attraction. All types of large and small fish abound. You will see large groupers (in particular Nassau, black, red hind and tiger) as well as relatively shy queen triggerfish, angelfish, scores of confident yellowtail snappers, crevalle jacks, horse-eye jacks

M KEIFE

Red hinds are also known as "speckled hinds" and "strawberry groupers."

Strange Ch-ch-ch-changes

Evolution and adaptation have culminated in some interesting abilities for groupers. Though they normally change their color during the transition stage from juvenile to adult, they may also temporarily change colors in defense when they are startled or as camouflage when moving from one site to another. Additionally, many groupers undergo unique changes in their sexual development: Members of the subfamily Epinephelinae (the largest grouper group) are born as females and can produce eggs when mature. Later, they change sex, be-

Large groupers may be over 50 years old.

coming functionally male. As a result, the only males in this grouper subfamily are the older, larger fish. It is important not to harm or fish for large grouper, because without them the species cannot reproduce.

and bar jacks. You may also see bull sharks here. Huge and surprisingly confident green moray eels have also made this site their home.

If you take a camera on this dive you'll have no shortage of subjects. The various fish species are easy to see and abundant.

36 Faisy

Nestled at 22m between two coral-covered pinnacles on a sandy bed are the remains of a patrol ship. Though this wreck is broken up, you can still distinguish the boat's stern. Small tropicals inhabit this area, as do a few parrotfish.

The pinnacles have a great deal of life on them. A look inside the basket sponges will reveal different types of worms (Christmas tree, fan and horseshoe), feather stars and soft corals growing on their walls.

The heads of the pinnacles (at 6-8m) also hold much of interest to the diver: gorgonians waving gently in the current, brightly colored snappers, trumpetfish, chromis, parrotfish, damselfish, grunts and basslets.

Location: Southwest of Cayo Anclitas

Depth Range: 6-22m (20-72ft)

Access: Boat

Expertise Rating: Novice

A trumpetfish rests in a colorful coral garden.

37 La Cueva del Pulpo

Start this dive at 20m, where 4m-high coral-covered mounds with many ledges, nooks and crannies are surrounded by sand. At their base are some colorful tube and basket sponges. Moray eels inhabit this area, as do squirrelfish, grunts, hamlets and even a few spotted drums.

This site is famous for its jewfish, including a particularly large one named "Chocolate" who frequents this and other sites close by. These robust (some might say ugly) creatures have no fear of divers. Keep your fingers close to you, or they might be mistaken for dinner!

Location: Southwest of Cayo Anclitas

Depth Range: 9-22m (30-72ft)

Access: Boat

Expertise Rating: Intermediate

Divers usually spend the first part of this dive exploring the base of the coral pinnacles and viewing the fish life before moving on to the cave from which this dive site gets its name.

Ascend to an open sandy area in the midst of coral (at 9m) to reach La Cueva del Pulpo ("Octopus' Cave"), which is big enough to enter. Its floor is a mix of mud and sand. Most divers exit the cave through the same opening that they enter by, though it is possible to leave through a short tunnel that ends at 18m. This cave is a particularly good spot to see resting turtles during a night dive.

Close to the cave are two large and attractive mountains of pillar coral. Move close to these imposing structures to find the colorful tropical fish nestling in their center.

French grunts are found under ledges at La Cueva del Pulpo.

Jewfish can reach a length of 2.5m.

38 Cabezo de Coral Negro

At 38m you'll find yourself above a coral-covered platform that has become a sharks' domain. This is a good site to encounter blacktip and bull sharks, which can be found circling the area's perimeter. Position yourself above the coral heads and watch the sharks' movements: The blacktip moves in a sleek and sharp manner, while the bull shark is less graceful. Though they will watch divers carefully, these creatures tend to maintain a respectful distance.

In keeping with the site's name, black coral grows just below the platform. As is common at most Jardines de la Reina

Location: South of Cayo Anclitas

Depth Range: 35-40m (115-131ft)

Access: Boat

Expertise Rating: Advanced

dive sites, you will see many yellowtail snapper. Other fish species seen here are crevalle jacks, bar jacks, groupers, gray snapper and gray angelfish, creole-fish and a few great barracuda. Silky sharks are also seen occasionally.

M KEIFE

A diver cautiously watches as a silky shark and crevalle jacks swim by.

Santiago de Cuba Dive Sites

Distinctive dive sites can be found both to the east and to the west of Santiago de Cuba, the country's second largest city, which sits on Cuba's eastern Caribbean shore. Here the island platform slopes down to 35m (115ft), where the ocean wall plummets straight down for more than 1,000m (3,300ft). Though diving is possible year-round, visibility is best from February to June. Water temperatures in this area are some of the island's warmest, ranging from 25° to 28°C (77° to 82°F). Land temperatures around Santiago can reach more than 32°C (90°F) during the month of August.

You can dive in this region from a number of bases, including Playa Sigua (east of Santiago de Cuba, approximately 30-45 minutes by road) and the SuperClubs Sierra Mar Hotel (near Chivirico, about an hour's drive west of Santiago de Cuba).

The underwater landscape consists of high buttes, channels and caves, and several wrecks are accessible to divers. The marine life is excellent: Angelfish, jacks, triggerfish and groupers inhabit these waters. Dolphins are a common sight here, though they keep their distance from divers.

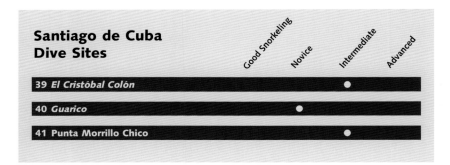

Santiago de Cuba Dive Sites	Good Snorkeling	Novice	Intermediate	Advanced
39 *El Cristóbal Colón*			●	
40 *Guarico*		●		
41 Punta Morrillo Chico			●	

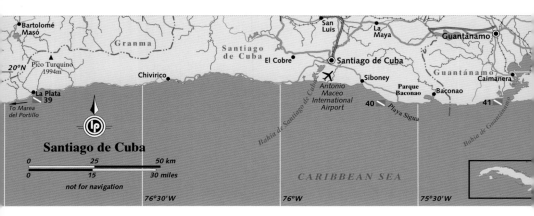

39 *El Cristóbal Colón*

As a wreck dive, *El Cristóbal Colón* strikes a nice balance between a well-preserved wreck with many features still observable and a lively artificial reef that many species call home.

Attacked at the battle of Santiago in 1898 during the Spanish-American war, this 6,800-ton armored cruiser was beached after an 80km chase by U.S. warships. The *Colón* was regarded as the finest vessel in the Spanish navy. It was also the most damaged by U.S. gunfire. Attempts to refloat her were soon abandoned due to the difficulty of the task.

The wreck is found close to shore. The ship's shallowest point is at 12m and the length of the wreck follows the seabed's incline down to 30m.

The *Colón* retains much of its original structure, though half of the wreck is now twisted on its starboard side. You can still see the engine room with its

Location: Near La Plata

Depth Range: 12-30m (40-98ft)

Access: Shore

Expertise Rating: Intermediate

heavy gears. The remainder of the hull is covered with a proliferation of colorful worms, hydroids and sponges. Tropical fish and schools of tarpon weave their way in and out of the wreck.

Although the wreck can be dived year-round, visibility is generally best during the drier months (February-June). During the rainy season, runoff from the Sierra Maestra mountains can hinder visibility. Take care not to stir the sandy bottom when diving on the *Colón*, as it would mar an extremely enjoyable dive.

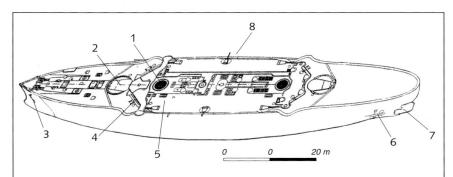

Though half of this wreck is now twisted on its starboard side, many of *El Cristóbal Colón's* features can still be observed:

1. conning tower and armored communication tube
2. barbette
3. anchor chain
4. diagonal armored bulkhead
5. ventilation frame
6. propeller shaft and bracket
7. steering gears
8. 15cm (6 inch) casemate position

40 *Guarico*

The *Guarico* is a small steel wreck that was sunk fairly recently. This wreck, resting on the sandy seafloor, has a tremendous amount of marine life on and around it. You'll see a large number of fire and fan

Location: South of Playa Sigua

Depth: 15m (50ft)

Access: Boat

Expertise Rating: Novice

G GOTERA

A grouper watches a diver investigate colorful coral and invertebrates on the *Guarico*.

worms, which increase the brilliance of a wreck already covered in colorful corals and sponges.

Around the wreck you are likely to see parrotfish, angelfish, groupers and jacks. There are many small tropical fish, in particular wrasse and gobies. Gobies are ardent fish cleaners and obtain a free meal of parasites for their services. It is also possible to see rays at this dive site.

41 Punta Morrillo Chico

Punta Morrillo Chico offers a fantastic diving experience close to shore that can be accessed by boat (approximately an hour from the dive base at Playa Sigua) or by road.

Near the shore, descend and swim west along the drop-off at 30m, ascending gradually. The amount of marine life at this site is phenomenal. Thousands of damselfish and a large number of green moray eels and groupers can be seen. The site is made even more colorful by

Location: West of the mouth of Bahía de Guantánamo

Depth: 30m (98ft)

Access: Shore or boat

Expertise Rating: Intermediate

the proliferation of conches, gorgonians and sponges.

Marea del Portillo

West of Santiago de Cuba, the Granma province juts into the Caribbean. This point, particularly around the Marea del Portillo area, offers diving opportunities for those seeking colorful and lively reefs, wrecks and walls. You can see small tropicals, barracuda, groupers and snappers in this region. This is also a good area for spotting dolphins.

Guardalavaca Dive Sites

Guardalavaca is an attractive beach resort that occupies a stretch of white-sand beach facing the Atlantic Ocean, close to the Sierra Maestra mountains. The beach, which is broken by promontories, has an intimate, tranquil feel.

Divers will find walls, caves, platforms and attractive terraces in this region, as well as a few wrecks.

Diving and snorkeling are not the only outdoor activities worth exploring in this area—deep-sea fishing, windsurfing, kayaking, sailing and bicycling are all available. The landscape here is verdant, with rolling hills and many small farms. However, during Cuba's May-October rainy season this is one of the driest parts of the country.

G GOTERA/CUBANACÁN

Small tropicals investigate a colorful leathery barrel sponge.

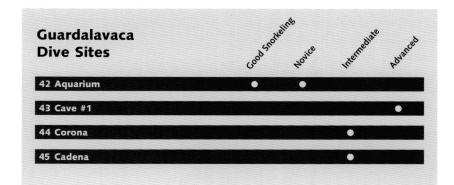

Guardalavaca Dive Sites	Good Snorkeling	Novice	Intermediate	Advanced
42 Aquarium	●	●		
43 Cave #1				●
44 Corona			●	
45 Cadena			●	

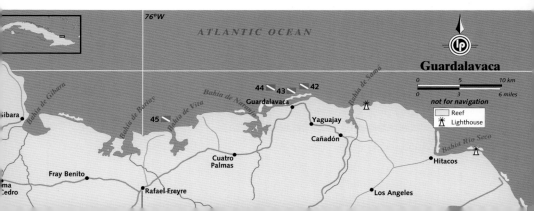

42 Aquarium

Though Aquarium is a popular name for dive sites throughout Cuba, it is particularly appropriate to apply it to this site near Guardalavaca, where you'll reliably see a wide variety of colorful marine life.

Location: Northeast of Guardalavaca

Depth Range: 10-15m (33-50ft)

Access: Boat

Expertise Rating: Novice

Start the dive at around 10m and follow the gentle slope down to 15m. Around the small, rocky, coral-covered outcrops you'll find butterflyfish, various types of angelfish, parrotfish, blue hamlets, tangs and—nesting in the nooks and crannies—cardinalfish and squirrelfish. You can also see a number of sponges, including tubes and vases.

43 Cave #1

This dive starts at 10-12m on a flat, sandy platform that is covered with soft corals and sea rods. Here you're likely to see swarms of blue chromis, blue parrotfish, gobies, jacks, butterflyfish and some solitary groupers. The seabed slopes gently to a ridge at about 35m, where you'll find greater coral cover and small sandy channels.

Location: North of Guardalavaca

Depth Range: 10-35m (33-115ft)

Access: Boat

Expertise Rating: Advanced

There is a cave at 20m. Use a flashlight to illuminate what it has to offer—swarms of glistening silver fingerlings, so many that you'll feel you are covered by them. You can exit through a small hole at the back of the cave. Again, take great care not to damage this environment by kicking the cave's walls with your fins.

On exiting the hole you'll be facing out to sea along the same ridge, where healthy blooms of black coral, huge plate corals, starlet coral and various other types of coral reside. Smaller caves, nooks and crannies are also abundant. Several types of snapper inhabit this area and you are also likely to see tiger, red, black and Nassau grouper.

U NATOLI

Groupers rest quietly on the seafloor.

44 Corona

The visibility along this extremely lively and colorful wall is excellent, doing justice to the bright coral, sponges and fish around you. You may see yellowtail snapper, ocean triggerfish, some tarpon and sharks (including blacktips) as you move along the wall.

Black coral is prevalent here, as are sponges, including rope sponges and large, brightly-colored encrusting sponges. If you look at the rope sponges closely, you will see that many are covered with small, flower-like zoanthids. In addition, you may find some brittle stars that have made the sponges their

Location: Northwest of Guardalavaca

Depth Range: 20-40m (66-130ft)

Access: Boat

Expertise Rating: Intermediate

home. This wall also supports a number of colorful tunicates.

On the platform before the drop-off you may see spotted eagle rays, which are known to cruise walls and sandy areas.

M KEIFE

At Corona you will find brightly colored and pristine rope sponges.

Prolific Porifera

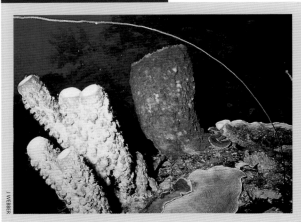

A wide variety of sponges (Phylum *Porifera*, meaning hole-bearing) are common throughout Cuba's waters. The most common types are vase, rope and barrel sponges—some of which can grow to over 2m (6ft). Sponges draw water, containing food and oxygen, into their interior through small holes called incurrent pores found all over the sponge. Once inside, the water is then pumped through the sponge tissue by the movement of whip-like extensions called flagella. At the same time, nutrients and oxygen are filtered out of the water into the sponge. The water then moves into the interior cavity and exits the sponge via one or more excurrent openings.

45 Cadena

This site is named Cadena ("Chain") after the huge tug boat chain found at 20m. This chain was dropped in 1962 and now rests on a series of large coral-covered outcrops, surrounded by sand.

Around a pinnacle of untouched coral you may find barracuda, gray angelfish, parrotfish, yellowtail snapper and jacks, as well as Christmas tree worms and other invertebrates. Various small- and medium-sized tropical fish abound in this region, as do oysters. Sponges are

Location: Northwest of Bahía de Vita

Depth: 20m (66ft)

Access: Boat

Expertise Rating: Intermediate

common, including barrel and vase sponges. Close to this site is another drop-off complete with deep-water gorgonians and black coral.

Santa Lucía Dive Sites

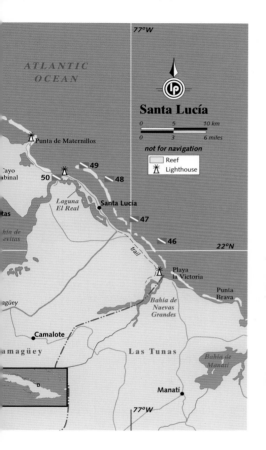

Santa Lucía beach serves as Camagüey province's primary tourist resort. Located on the Atlantic shore 180km (112 miles) northeast of Camagüey, it provides the diver with many possibilities: Dive attractive reefs, explore the *Mortera* and other wrecks, and view pelagic fish and sharks. Though the area around Santa Lucía is flat and uninspiring, the resort has much to offer. The waters are warm and the 20km- (12.5-mile-) long beach is one of Cuba's most extensive.

CUBANACÁN

The beach at Santa Lucía.

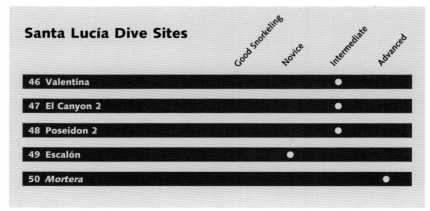

Santa Lucía Dive Sites	Good Snorkeling	Novice	Intermediate	Advanced
46 Valentina			●	
47 El Canyon 2			●	
48 Poseidon 2			●	
49 Escalón		●		
50 *Mortera*				●

46 Valentina

A sharply sloping platform covered with hard and soft corals leads you to a sandy bed at 30m. Snappers and hamlets are common here. You may also see pufferfish, groupers and (if you are lucky) even sea turtles. At the end of the platform is a steep wall covered with several species of colorful corals and sponges.

This is one of the best sites to see southern stingrays, spotted eagle rays and mantas. The spotted eagle ray and the southern stingray can reach a width of 152cm and 229cm respectively. The

Location: Northwest of the mouth of Bahía de Nuevas Grandes

Depth: 30m (98ft)

Access: Boat

Expertise Rating: Intermediate

somewhat larger manta can attain a width of 670cm. Whether alone or in small groups, rays never fail to capture the attention of divers.

47 El Canyon 2

This site gets its name from the large coral-covered canyons that slope toward the sea wall. You can see a spectacular amount of life here, including schools of brightly colored tropical fish and sponges of all different colors and varieties.

The canyons have attractive rocky overhangs covered in soft corals, algae

Location: Southeast of Santa Lucía

Depth: 20m (66ft)

Access: Boat

Expertise Rating: Intermediate

A diver enjoys the coral gardens of El Canyon 2.

and smaller sponges (prevalent where the canyons meet the wall). Schools of snappers, hamlets, bass and bar jacks also inhabit this area.

The wall has some surprises, including brightly colored whips, corals, huge orange sponges and blooms of black coral at 26m. At a similar depth you will find several small caves, some of which you can enter. Many of these caves are home to small silverside fish, which favor dark recesses. The tops of these caves are covered with sea rods, soft corals and fans.

48 Poseidon 2

Poseidon 2 is the name given to this stunning coral garden, found on a platform at 18m. From the platform, the seabed slopes gently down toward the wall, where marine life is found in abundance.

This is an excellent site to take photographs because many of the marine creatures are not shy. In addition to the tropicals commonly found at Cuba's dive sites, here you will find groupers and tarpon, both of which will move closer to watch slow-moving divers. The dense

Location: North of Santa Lucía

Depth Range: 18-30m (60-98ft)

Access: Boat

Expertise Rating: Intermediate

coral growth covered with gorgonians, invertebrates and fish is a further incentive for photographers.

49 Escalón

A long, wide sandy ledge runs along the top of a wall at 20m. The incredible life found along this wall makes for a very beautiful dive. This ledge is home to a variety of orange sponges, sea fingers and small corals. Their range of colors is spectacular. While moving west you may see diverse fish life, including schools of snappers and blue chromis.

Location: Northeast of the mouth of Bahía de Nuevitas

Depth Range: 20-30m (66-100ft)

Access: Boat

Expertise Rating: Novice

This is a good site to see angelfish, including queen and blue angelfish, as well as hogfish and puffers. The water of this region appears bright blue and as you look out to sea it is possible to see larger species like tarpon and barracuda.

When diving Escalón you are likely to see various types of angelfish, like this gray angelfish.

J WEBBER

50 *Mortera*

This Spanish merchant ship sunk under unfortunate circumstances in 1896. Shortly after leaving Havana, the *Mortera* collided with a warship. Nevertheless, the captain decided to continue the journey along the coast. On nearing Bahía de Nuevitas he realized that the ship's damage was greater than he first thought and that repairs were needed. Unfortunately, strong currents in the Nuevitas Channel made entry difficult for the ailing ship, and she sank in the mouth of the bay.

The wreck, resting at 8-27m between Playa Santa Lucía and Cayo Sabinal, is now home to a variety of marine life. Lying at a slant, its metal sides are covered with mollusks, colorful corals, algae, gorgonians and sponges.

Inside the ship it is difficult to identify the original structural parts due to the profusion of coral growth. Small invertebrates found here include feather dusters, hydroids and Christmas tree worms.

Location: Mouth of Bahía de Nuevitas

Depth Range: 8-27m (26-88ft)

Access: Boat

Expertise Rating: Advanced

Fish life in and around the ship includes snooks, red snappers and large gray snappers. You are also likely to see bull sharks near the ship's stern.

It is possible to enter the ship in some places but you must be careful to take the usual precautions to prevent damage to the site: Ensure that your equipment is not left dangling and keep kicking to a minimum in order not to damage the luxuriant coral.

At times the current in this area is strong, though dive operators don't normally visit the site when this is the case.

D DOOLEY

Feather dusters make the Mortera wreck their home.

Cayo Coco Dive Sites

Cayo Coco is the main tourist island in the Archipiélago de Camagüey. It is just 100km (62 miles) northeast of Ciego de Ávila and a three-hour drive west from Santa Lucía. Unlike most Cuban cayes, Cayo Coco is accessible by car via the 27km- (15 mile-) long causeway that crosses over the Bahía de Perros.

This 370-sq-km (143-sq-mile) coral caye is about 37km (23 miles) long, with white sandy beaches running along the Atlantic side. The interior is heavily forested and the whole island is a wildlife refuge that is home to many seabirds, including pelicans and flamingos.

It is not surprising that the diving around this island is spectacular. Cayo Coco's clear waters provide excellent conditions for marine-world observation. The density of marine life is good and you are likely to spot a variety of large and small fish within the reefs.

M KEIFE

Nurse sharks often lie below overhangs.

Cayo Coco Dive Sites	Good Snorkeling	Novice	Intermediate	Advanced
51 El Peñón			●	
52 La Jaula 1, 2, 3 & 4			●	

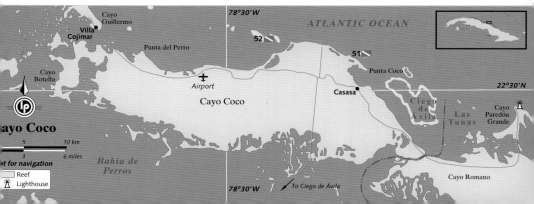

51 El Peñón

Upon reaching the seabed you'll find patch reefs nearly a meter high. Coral cover is rich and dense. Gold, beige, brown and purple-colored soft coral, deep-water gorgonians and sea rods abound. Hard corals include fungus, brain, leaf and star. You will also see many healthy examples of encrusting and tube sponges.

Amid this lush coral scene you will likely see coral-inhabiting fish species: Barracuda, ocean triggerfish, surgeonfish,

Location: North of Punta Coco

Depth: 20m (66ft)

Access: Boat

Expertise Rating: Intermediate

gray angelfish, margates, cubera snappers, conies, tiger groupers, African pompanos and southern stingrays can all be found in this area. Smaller fish species include blue chromis and butterflyfish.

52 La Jaula 1, 2, 3 & 4

La Jaula is divided into four distinct areas numbered 1, 2, 3 and 4. Each allows the diver to experience the attractive coral formations found along Cayo Coco's reef. Abundant star coral (a principle reef builder) is found at all of the sites, as are gorgonians and small to medium-sized sponges. The fish species you are likely to see and the size of the coral formations differ somewhat at each La Jaula area.

La Jaula 1, at 28m, is one of the better places to see eagle rays, nurse sharks, tarpon and large snappers. Moray eels and turtles also inhabit these waters.

Location: North of Cayo Coco

Depth Range: 15-30m (50-100ft)

Access: Boat

Expertise Rating: Intermediate

La Jaula 2 and 3 are located at 30m and 17m respectively. In these areas of the marine platform, you are likely to see snappers, tarpon and perhaps even reef sharks. The coral formations here are not as large as those at La Jaula 1, so the area feels more open. Both La Jaula 2 and 3 have similar characteristics, but La Jaula 3 has a greater density of gorgonians.

La Jaula 4 is a shallower dive at about 15m. Here you'll see large, colorful striped and rainbow parrotfish, as well as bar jacks moving around large coral boulders. You may see spotted moray eels in small holes between the coral heads. Larger holes contain many fish, including snappers and grunts.

D WILLIAMS

This scene is typical of Cayo Coco's waters.

Varadero Dive Sites

Varadero is on Cuba's north shore, just 140km (87 miles) east of Havana. Its pristine white-sand beaches contrast with the bright turquoise sea for the 20km (13 mile) stretch. The area is well known for its scuba diving—with over 30 dive sites to choose from, it is the perfect place to take a beach or dive vacation. In addition, Varadero's gentle currents provide safe and enjoyable diving for both new and experienced divers.

Several local companies offer dive packages that can include a trip to the inland Saturno Caves, shipwreck dives (like Barco Hundido and Barco Patrullero) and a trip to Playa Girón (due south of Varadero on the Caribbean coast).

D WILLIAMS

Varadero's white-sand beaches occasionally tempt divers out of the water.

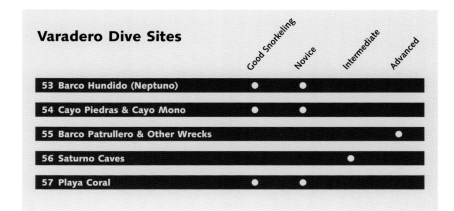

Varadero Dive Sites

	Good Snorkeling	Novice	Intermediate	Advanced
53 Barco Hundido (Neptuno)	●	●		
54 Cayo Piedras & Cayo Mono	●	●		
55 Barco Patrullero & Other Wrecks				●
56 Saturno Caves			●	
57 Playa Coral	●	●		

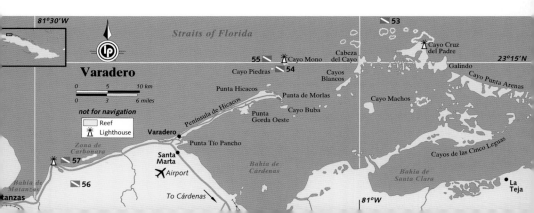

53 Barco Hundido (Neptuno)

This site is known as both Barco Hundido ("Sunken Ship") and Neptuno. Its prime feature is a 40m-long boat sunk in the 1940s. The boat is now home to several eels. Most are green morays (some reaching a length of almost 2m), though there are also a few purplemouth morays.

Location: Northeast of Cayos Blancos

Depth: 10m (33ft)

Access: Boat

Expertise Rating: Novice

This wreck is a good place to see groupers, triggerfish, angelfish, spadefish, cubera snappers, rock beauties, butterflyfish and even porcupinefish. There are many excellent opportunities for novice photographers to practice their shots because of the good visibility, intensity of light, variety of life and color that the area offers. The current at this site is usually mild.

G GOTERA

Divers explore Barco Hundido (Neptuno).

54 Cayo Piedras and Cayo Mono

A one-hour boat ride from Varadero beach takes you to Cayo Piedras, where you can undertake both shallow and deep dives. Around the islet, at 10m, you will find many tropical fish: damselfish, various types of chromis, tangs, bass and barracuda. Star and brain coral are common.

At Cayo Mono, northeast of Cayo Piedras, you will see many soft corals (including corky sea fingers, sea rods and venus sea fans) and sponges. The fish are similar to those at Cayo Piedras. Grunts, including French and bluestripes, are found in great number, as are wrasse,

Location: North of Punta de Morlas

Depth Range: 6-10m (20-33ft)

Access: Boat

Expertise Rating: Novice

snappers and damselfish. It is also possible to spot hogfish and triggerfish. Occasionally you can find nurse sharks lying on the sand under ledges in this region, though they are not seen in great numbers.

D DOOLEY

Blue chromis usually swim in the midwater above reefs and feed on plankton.

55 Barco Patrullero & Other Wrecks

As a way of developing the diving possibilities in the area, authorities sunk four boats and one airplane near Varadero in the late 1990s. They are arranged roughly in a circle.

The largest and most imposing of the wrecks is called Barco Patrullero, a 97m-long patrol ship found at the 3 o'clock

Location: North of Punta Hicacos

Depth Range: 15-30m (50-100ft)

Access: Boat

Expertise Rating: Advanced

position in the circle of wrecks. This 1945 Koni-class Russian patrol ship was used by the Cuban navy in the 1980s. Reportedly, it cost US$200,000 to prepare the ship for her final resting place. All traces of oil were removed and modifications were made (such as opening up spaces that could trap a diver) to make this ship diver-friendly.

The bottom of Barco Patrullero's hull rests at 28m. As you approach the stern, you'll have a clear view of the ship's surface-to-air missiles and some guns. You can enter Barco Patrullero and peer through open portholes at several points while moving along the ship's rail. Photo opportunities include views that capture the sharp edges and stark gray of the ship, penetrate the ship's

The Barco Patrullero was cleaned and prepared for divers before it was scuttled.

interior (which contains old electrical boxes) and reach through to the brightly lit blue sea on the other side.

The number of the ship (383) can still be seen, and the name "Che" has been inscribed on her. Move along the ship to see 30mm and 57mm guns on the prow and some smoke dispensers originally used to confuse the enemy as to the position of the ship.

Different types of snappers and small tropicals will likely be seen swimming around the boat. Because this ship was sunk recently, there is little in the way of coral and sponge

Barco Patrullero is in excellent condition.

growth. Nevertheless, many parts of it are now covered with white hydroids and small anemones. It is hoped Barco Patrullero and the other wrecks will soon become lively and colorful artificial reefs.

Missiles and guns on Barco Patrullero.

Other Wrecks

Circling clockwise from Barco Patrullero, you will find the *Coral Negro*, the *Remocador*, a Russian airplane and *La Cohetera*.

The 45m-long protocol ship *Coral Negro*, found at 20m, functioned for a time as a bar and restaurant, then was intentionally scuttled in 1995. Also found at 20m is the tug boat *Remocador*. The small airplane found at 15m (a Russian AN 24) was used by the Cuban army as a transport plane. Upon entering the plane, most divers instinctively head for the cockpit, placing themselves where the pilot's seat would have been. Farther along on the circuit is *La Cohetera*, at 18m. This was once a patrol boat and still has its firing mechanisms.

Like Barco Patrullero, these relatively new wrecks lack developed coral, sponge and fish communities. Clearly, however, the wrecks have added to Varadero's diving attraction, which will increase as marine life overtakes these structures.

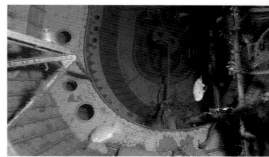

Inside the Russian AN 24 airplane.

56 Saturno Caves

Saturno Caves is a series of connected inland freshwater caves 18km from Varadero. To get there, take the highway out of Varadero toward Matanzas and make a left onto the first road (toward the Varadero airport). After 1.5km, take another left to the parking lot. A small path seemingly in the middle of nowhere leads down to the immense, deep main pool of the Saturno Caves. The water here is amazingly clear—and cold. Come prepared with a wetsuit.

This dive is worth preparing for, as it is very different from the warm-water

Location: 18km (11 miles) southwest of Varadero

Depth: 20m (66ft)

Access: Road

Expertise Rating: Intermediate

ocean diving that is common in Cuba. In this series of caves you will see beautiful stalactites and stalagmites. Blind fish also inhabit these waters.

Though most divers are satisfied with spending time in the large pool viewing rock formations and fish, more experienced cave divers may want to explore the tunnels that lead to other chambers. Such exploration should only be undertaken by suitably trained divers with an experienced guide.

Diving here will give you a glimpse of Cuban life away from the tourist resorts: Young Cubans visit the cave to swim and enjoy the cool atmosphere.

57 Playa Coral

Playa Coral is one of the main dive sites along the Zona de Carbonera, an area fronted by a 2km-long reef that begins close to the mouth of the Bahía de Matanzas, 20km from the start of the Península de Hicacos-Varadero. The entry point for this dive, which can be accessed from shore, is a 20-minute drive from Varadero. People who want to dive the wall should access the site by boat.

This reef has many channels that descend to a wall at 2-8m. As you move along the channels you'll see many species of coral including elkhorn, staghorn and scroll. There are also a number of soft corals and sea fans, as well as sponges.

Location: Near shore approximately 20km (12 miles) west of Varadero

Depth Range: 2-8m (6-26ft)

Access: Shore or boat

Expertise Rating: Novice

Although this is a relatively easy, shallow dive, both novice and experienced divers should find it interesting and colorful. Large numbers of parrotfish can be seen, as well as cornetfish, trumpetfish, basslets and blue chromis. Black coral and deep-water gorgonians can be found in deeper waters along the wall.

Staghorn coral, sponges and soft corals are commonly found at Playa Coral.

Havana Area Dive Sites

In addition to its historic and cultural attractions, Havana offers surprisingly enjoyable diving, including wrecks, walls and reefs. Diving takes place in two main areas: to the east (Playas del Este and the Tarará Marina) and to the west (Barlovento, using Marina Hemingway and Villa Cocomar as dive bases) of central Havana.

In Havana's waters you can find a variety of tropical fish, rays, colorful corals and sponges and even a few shipwrecks. Most dive sites are reached by boat.

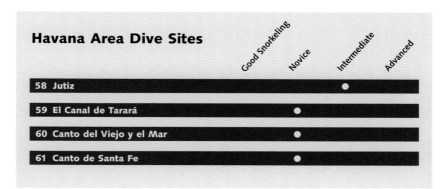

Havana Area Dive Sites	Good Snorkeling	Novice	Intermediate	Advanced
58 Jutiz			●	
59 El Canal de Tarará		●		
60 Canto del Viejo y el Mar		●		
61 Canto de Santa Fe		●		

58 Jutiz

This dive begins at 20m on a sandy bed with small coral outcrops. As you head east, the outcrops become larger and are more vibrant. You will need to navigate through coral-covered pinnacles as the seabed slopes gently downward. The corals in this area include fungus, cactus, leaf and star corals.

Christmas tree, feather duster and fan worms are just a few of the invertebrates living in the area. You will also find sponges such as the delicate lilac vase, yellow tube and large basket sponges.

Fish you are likely to see (though not in great numbers) include puffer-fish, angelfish and even spotted drums.

Location: North of Playa Santa María del Mar

Depth Range: 18-30m (60-98ft)

Access: Boat

Expertise Rating: Intermediate

Smaller reef fish common to this area include yellowhead wrasse, blueheads, basslets and blue chromis.

As you circle west at 18m (back to the entry point), the underwater landscape takes on an almost golden hue due to an increase in sea rods and sea fingers. Here you will see many small tropicals weaving their way around attractive soft corals.

M KEIFE

You'll see delicate vase sponges while diving Jutiz.

59 El Canal de Tarará

You'll begin this dive at 7m, above a sandy bed covered with gorgonians and sea rods. Head east to arrive at a small coral-covered bank that reaches 15m. A vast expanse of sand extends from the bank's base at 17m.

As you head south along the bank, you may spot sea spiders, morays and bryozoans in small crevices. The wall itself has an abundance of corals. Orange- and rose-colored encrusting sponges abound. You are likely to see trumpetfish, hamlets, jacks, butterfly-fish, chromis and barracuda.

Location: North of the Boca de Tarará

Depth Range: 7-17m (23-56ft)

Access: Boat

Expertise Rating: Novice

Another unusual species that you'll find in this area is the sharksucker, which attaches itself to sharks and other large fish using a disc-shaped sucker on the top of its head. They are dark with a thin white stripe from nose to tail. In El Canal de Tarará you may see them swimming sans shark over coral reefs.

60 Canto del Viejo y el Mar

As with Canto de Santa Fe, the best parts of this dive are along a small coral-covered bank whose base is at 16m. On and along the bottom of the bank are many sponges, particularly large brown basket sponges, some of which reach 1-1.5m high.

Location: North of Marina Hemingway

Depth: 16m (52ft)

Access: Boat

Expertise Rating: Novice

The bank's crevices contain several species of worms and hydroids, as well as white-tipped sea urchins. A few moray eels also inhabit this area. You are likely to see many species of small fish, including damselfish, yellowhead and bluehead wrasse, blackbar soldierfish and ocean triggerfish.

Leave the bottom of the bank and ascend to a platform covered with sea fingers, sea rods and some wavy tree coral.

D WILLIAMS

Blackbar soldierfish may swim upside-down in caves.

61 Canto de Santa Fe

At Canto de Santa Fe the seabed drops sharply from 16m to 20m in the form of a stair or bank. At the bottom lies an extensive sandy bed with small coral-covered outcrops. Head northeast along the bank. You are likely to see fan worms, Christmas tree worms and different types of hydroids. Look in crevices and small holes to discover spotted morays and lobsters.

There are a few small caves where the bank meets the sandy bed that are often inhabited by schools of grunts, glasseye snappers, schoolmasters, soldierfish and squirrelfish. Other fish species that you

Location: North of Marina Hemingway

Depth Range: 16-20m (53-66ft)

Access: Boat

Expertise Rating: Novice

are likely to see on this dive include trunkfish and parrotfish.

This is a particularly good area to see small yellow stingrays, which blend in with the sand around the coral-covered outcrops at the base of the stair. Your main clue to their presence is their large bulbous eyes. Your approach may prompt them to move, enabling you to get a good glimpse of one in its entirety—mottled, brown nearly-round body and wispy (yet relatively short) tail.

Yellow stingrays attract their prey by raising the front of their disc-like bodies to form a tunnel that looks like a shelter. Fish enter with a false sense of security, only to become the ray's meal. Fish aren't the only animals that should beware of these well-camouflaged rays. They can inflict a painful wound with the spine at the base of their tail if stepped on or carelessly handled by divers.

D WILLIAMS

Attractive coral outcrop at Canto de Santa Fe.

Cayo Levisa

Drive about 100km (62 miles) west of Havana to arrive at the jumping-off point for Cayo Levisa. This caye, just off the north coast of the Pinar del Río province, offers divers a chance to see the usual array of tropicals as well as several species of snapper, sea bass and grouper in a remote, pristine environment. Lobsters are also common in these waters, and you may see eagle rays and stingrays.

Marine Life

Cuba's marine world is rich with variety and color. The waters around this island are home to hundreds of different fish and invertebrate animals, many of which are associated with coral reef environments.

Following are photos of some common vertebrates and invertebrates you will encounter around the island. The name below each photo represents the common name. The two-part scientific name

G GOTERA/CUBANACÁN

appears in italics. The first word is the Genus. The second is the Species. Where species identification is uncertain, either the Family (F.) or Phylum (Ph.) name is given.

Common Fish

balloonfish
Diodon holocanthus

blue chromis
Chromis cyanea

bluestriped grunt
Haemulon sciurus

blue tang
Acanthurus coeruleus

bridled goby
Coryphopterus glaucofraenum

creole wrasse
Clepticus parrae

dusky squirrelfish
Holocentrus vexillarius

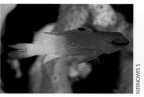

fairy basslet
Gramma loreto

French grunt
Haemulon flavolineatum

gray angelfish
Pomacanthus arcuatus

horse-eye jack
Caranx latus

jewfish
Epinephelus itajara

Nassau grouper
Epinephelus striatus

red hind
Epinephelus guttatus

sharknose goby
Gobiosoma evelynae

sharksucker
Echeneis naucrates

spinyhead blenny
Acanthemblemaria spinosa

spotted goatfish
Pseudupeneus maculatus

stoplight parrotfish
Sparisoma viride

tarpon
Megalops atlanticus

trumpetfish
Aulostomus maculatus

yellowhead wrasse
Halichoeres garnoti

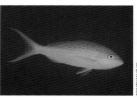

yellowtail snapper
Ocyurus chrysurus

whale shark
Rhincodon typus

Common Invertebrates

barrel sponge
Xestospongia muta

basket star
Astrophyton muricatum

branching sponge
Ph. *Porifera*

butterprint brain coral
Meandrina meandrites

Caribbean spiny lobster
Panulirus argus

Christmas tree worm
Spirobranchus giganteus

closed-valley brain coral
Colpophyllia breviseralis

flamingo tongue
Cyphoma gibbosum

elkhorn coral
Acropora palmata

encrusting gorgonian
Erythropodium caribaeorum

feather duster (fanworm)
F. *Sabellidae*

five-toothed sea cucumber
Actinopygia agassizii

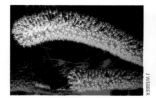

knobby sea rods
Eunicea clavigera

vase sponge
Ph. *Porifera*

venus sea fan
Gorgonia flabellum

Hazardous Marine Life

Most stings and scrapes result when a diver accidentally bumps into coral or touches a creature that instinctively tries to defend itself. Respect for the marine world, good buoyancy control and the use of common sense will prevent most marine life injuries while diving.

Some wounds are painful but relatively harmless, while others may require medical attention. Carefully assess each situation to determine the best course of action. Avoid contact with the following:

Fire Coral

M LAWRENCE

Fire coral grows in a variety of shapes and colors, often in colonies composed of finger-like columns with whitish tips. The entire colony is covered by tiny pores and fine, hair-like projections nearly invisible to the unaided eye. Fire coral may encrust and take the form of a variety of reef structures, which makes it difficult to identify by colony shape.

Fire corals "sting" by discharging small, specialized cells called nematocysts. Contact causes a burning sensation that lasts for several minutes and may produce red welts on the skin. Do not rub the area, as you will spread the stinging particles. Cortisone cream can reduce the inflammation and antihistamine cream is good for killing the pain.

Sea Urchins

Sea urchins are found in greatest numbers at shallow depths. Some species are inactive by day, but emerge from crevices at night to forage for plant material. Sea urchins have sharp spines that break off easily and are left in the wound. These may cause infection if not properly

S SIMONSEN

treated. Minor punctures can be treated by removing the spine or spines and using an antibiotic ointment. Seek a doctor's advice for more serious wounds.

Fire (or Bristle) Worms

S SIMONSEN

Fire worms, which are found on reefs throughout Cuba, are a mobile relative of the sedentary feather duster and Christmas tree worms. In fire worms, the tiny bristles are sharp and venomous and, if touched, remain within the resulting wound. This causes a painful, burning sensation and may result in welts.

Sponges

They may be beautiful, but sponges can also pack a powerful punch with fine spicules that sting on contact. Differentiating between sponges can be a difficult task. Bright red sponges often carry the most potent sting but are not the only culprits. If you touch a stinging sponge, carefully scrape the area with the edge of a sharp knife. Cortisone cream may help reduce pain and swelling.

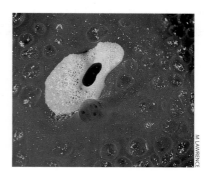

Scorpionfish

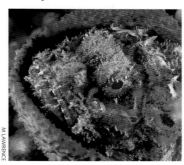

Scorpionfish are well camouflaged and difficult to spot—they look more like a plant-covered rock than a fish. They have poisonous spines hidden along their fins. If you practice good buoyancy control and watch where you put your hands, you shouldn't have a problem with them. If you get stung, go to a doctor as soon as possible because the sting can result in a severe allergic reaction, great pain and infection.

Sea Bather's Eruption

Often incorrectly called "sea lice," this skin irritation is actually caused by the stings of larval sea anemones, usually on covered areas of the body. Symptoms include itching, burning and red splotches on your skin that can last for several days. These larval anemones seem to be more prominent in the spring months. To minimize irritation, scrub thoroughly with soap and water and use a decontaminant such as papain or vinegar. Cortisone cream can relieve some of the discomfort.

Stingrays

The southern stingray (with pointed snout and wing tips) and the yellow stingray (with rounded snout and wing tips) are common in Cuba's waters. Stingrays generally stay along the sandy sea floor and are harmless unless you disturb them. They can lash out with one or two venomous spines at the base of their long tails, inflicting a painful wound that can easily get infected. If you get stung, go to the hospital immediately.

Barracuda

Barracuda have an un- deserved reputation for aggression. Though they can be curious, they are usually shy of divers and aren't aggressive unless they feel attacked. Don't irritate them and they won't irritate you.

Eels

Recognized by their long, thick, snake-like bodies and tapered heads, eels won't bother you unless you bother them. To breathe prop- erly, they must constantly open and close their mouths—this is not a threat. If you do get bitten by an eel, don't try to pull away, as their teeth are very sharp. Allow the eel to release its grip, then surface safe- ly and head to the nearest hospital for treatment.

Sharks

Most of the sharks you will encounter in Cuba are not aggressive, as long as you adopt a "look but don't touch" policy. The few shark attacks that do occur generally happen when divers are spearfishing. Snorkelers and swimmers may have a higher risk of being injured by a shark. If a shark bites, treat the vic- tim for both the wound and for shock. Minor cuts can be treated with an antibacterial ointment. For more severe wounds, stop the bleeding by applying pressure and trans- port the victim to a hospital.

Basic First-Aid Procedures

The measures described below are basic first aid using commonly available materials and equipment and are not a substitute for medical attention. The seriousness of an encounter with a hazardous marine animal depends not only on the nature of the animal but on the location of the wound—a bite, spine or sting near the eyes should be treated differently than one to a callused heel.

1. Immediately, in the water if possible, check that the victim is breathing. If not, clear the airway and begin mouth-to-mouth resuscitation. Remove the victim from the water as quickly as possible, check for breathing and heartbeat and begin CPR if necessary.

2. To minimize shock, place the victim in a head-down position; minimize blood loss by applying pressure and elevate the limb involved.

3. Try to remove spicules, spines or bristles with tweezers or adhesive tape, but leave any that are deeply embedded or are in joints, near eyes or near major blood vessels for surgical removal later. Wash the area with sterile (boiled) water. If a sponge is thought to be involved, soak the area with vinegar diluted with an equal volume of sterile water. Pain may be reduced by heating the afflicted area with warm water or a hot hair dryer.

4. If a creature with nematocysts was involved, the sting should be washed out with sea water. (Do not use fresh water, as nematocysts will trigger in defense of something "unnatural" to them; fresh water may in fact result in additional stings.) Flood the area with diluted vinegar and remove any visible nematocysts with a pair of tweezers. Apply shaving cream to the site and carefully scrape it with a razor or knife. Flood the area again with diluted vinegar. Make sure nematocysts are not spread to other areas—especially the eyes—or to other people.

5. Apply a topical antibiotic such as bacitracin or neomycin if available. Place a sterile dressing over the wound—a section cut from a clean cotton T-shirt or washcloth, boiled and then dried will do fine—and secure it with tape or string.

Dive Conservation & Awareness

To date, Cuba has not established any marine parks through legislation; however, plans are underway for parks in some areas including Cabo Francés (Isla de la Juventud), Varadero (Cayo Piedras, Cayo Mono and the Península de Hicacos) and the Guanahacabibes area (incorporating María la Gorda).

A few diving areas (Jardines de la Reina and Guajimico) have obtained licenses from the Ministry of Fisheries to regulate fishing. In the case of Jardines de la Reina, for example, the Ministry of Fisheries receives money from the fishing and dive boat operator for each visitor to the area. The money is used to fund enforcement of the regulation.

Fishing is also prohibited in Isla de la Juventud's diving areas, where a company is employed to ensure compliance. Other dive areas are currently seeking licenses to limit fishing within their diving areas.

Though diving areas can be preserved through the regulation and limitation of fishing, the needs of the local people should not be ignored. In a country where there are often food shortages, fishing is a necessary food source. Clearly, a balance must be achieved between meeting the needs of the people and protecting the marine environment. While regulations that forbid fishing in certain areas are a step in the right direction, a sustainable system that acknowledges both social and environmental factors (incorporating the zoning of both diving and fishing) is needed. Hopefully, the future establishment of marine parks will allow for this.

Responsible Diving

The popularity of diving is placing immense pressure on many sites, which tend to be located where the reefs and walls display the most beautiful corals and sponges. It only takes a moment—an inadvertently placed hand or a careless brush or kick with a fin—to destroy this fragile, living part of our delicate ecosystem. Please consider the following suggestions when diving:

1. Never drop boat anchors onto a coral reef and take care not to ground boats on coral. Encourage dive operators and regulatory bodies in their efforts to establish permanent moorings at dive sites.

2. Practice and maintain proper buoyancy control and avoid overweighting. Be aware that buoyancy can change over the period of an extended trip: Initially you may breathe harder and need more weight; a few days later you may breathe more

easily and need less weight. Be careful about buoyancy loss: As you go deeper, your wetsuit compresses and you lose buoyancy.

3. Avoid touching living marine organisms with your body or dragging equipment across the reef. Polyps can be damaged by even the gentlest contact. Never stand on coral, even if it looks solid and robust. The use of gloves is no longer recommended: It makes it too easy to hold on to the reef and the abrasion caused by gloves may be more damaging to the reef than your hands are. If you must hold on to the reef, touch only exposed rock or dead coral.

4. Be conscious of your fins. Even without contact, the surge from heavy fin strokes near the reef can do damage. Avoid full-leg kicks when working close to the bottom and when leaving a photo scene. When you inadvertently kick something, stop kicking! It seems obvious, but some divers either panic or are completely oblivious when they bump something. When treading water in shallow reef areas, take care not to kick up clouds of sand. Settling sand can easily smother the delicate organisms of the reef.

5. Attach all dangling gauges, computer consoles and octopus regulators to your BC. These are like miniature wrecking balls to a reef.

6. When swimming in strong currents, be especially careful about leg kicks and handholds.

7. Photographers must be extra careful. Cameras and equipment affect buoyancy. Changing f-stops, framing a subject and maintaining position for a photo often conspire to prohibit the ideal "no-touch" approach on a reef. When you must use "holdfasts," choose them intelligently (i.e., use only one finger for leverage off an area of dead coral).

8. Resist the temptation to collect or buy corals or shells. Aside from the ecological damage, taking home marine souvenirs depletes the beauty of a site and spoils the enjoyment of others.

9. Be sure to take home all your trash and any litter you may find as well. Plastics in particular are a serious threat to marine life.

10. Resist the temptation to feed fish. You may disturb their normal eating habits, encourage aggressive behavior or feed them food that is detrimental to their health.

Marine Conservation Organizations

Reefs and oceans are facing unprecedented environmental pressures. The following U.S.-based groups are actively involved in promoting responsible diving practices, publicizing environmental threats and lobbying for better policies.

CORAL: The Coral Reef Alliance
☎ 510-848-0110
www.coral.org

Coral Forest
☎ 415-788-REEF
www.blacktop.com /coralforest

Cousteau Society
☎ 757-523-9335
www.cousteausociety.org

Project AWARE Foundation
☎ 714-540-0251
www.projectaware.org

ReefKeeper International
☎ 305-358-4600
www.reefkeeper.org

Reef Relief
☎ 305-294-3100
www.reefrelief.org

Listings

Telephone Calls

To call Cuba, dial the international access code of the country you are calling from (011 from the U.S.), + 53 (Cuba's country code), + the city or area code (in parenthesis in these listings), + the three- to six-digit local number. Be forewarned that many numbers are being changed as the phone system is modernized.

Throughout Cuba, the information number is 113 during business hours. To reach the operator, dial 110. Emergency numbers include: 115 to call the fire department, 116 to call the police, and 118 to call an ambulance. Remember, they speak only Spanish.

Accommodations

The following hotels are listed by dive region. In popular tourist areas (such as Havana and Varadero) there are many hotels to choose from. Only those that can cater to divers or are affiliated with a dive shop are included. Nearly all provide rooms with private bath, air conditioning and phone.

María la Gorda

Hotel María la Gorda
(24 rooms)
Playa María la Gorda, Península de Guanahacabibes, Pinar del Río
☎ (04) 3121
Restaurant and bar; credit cards not accepted

Isla de la Juventud

Hotel Colony
(54 rooms, 23 cabañas)
Carretera de la Siguanea, km 41, Colony, Isla de la Juventud
☎ (61) 9-8282 fax: (61) 33-5212
Restaurant and bar; swimming pool; car rental; sports equipment rental; fridge in room

Cayo Largo

Isla del Sur Hotel Complex
(305 rooms)
Between Playa Linda Mar and Playa Blanca, Cayo Largo del Sur, Archipiélago de los Canarreos, Isla de la Juventud
☎ (5) 4-8111 fax: (5) 4-8201

6-hotel complex includes Villa Capricho, Villa Iguana, Villa Coral, Villa Soledad, Isla del Sur and Pelícano Hotel; restaurants and bars; swimming pools; sports equipment rental

Playa Girón

Hotel Horizontes Playa Girón
(292 rooms)
Gran Parque Natural Monteman, Playa Girón, Matanzas
☎ (59) 4118 fax: (59) 4117
www.horizontes.cu/playa/hoteles_de_playa
Restaurant, café and bar; disco; swimming pool; car and bike rental; tourist info

Cienfuegos, Guajimico & Trinidad

Hotel Ancón
(279 rooms)
Carretera a María Aguilar, Península de Ancón, Trinidad, Sancti Spíritus
☎ (419) 4011 fax: (667) 7424
Restaurants, café and bar; disco; post office; car rental

Hotel Costa Sur
(131 rooms)
Playa María Aguilar, Casilda, Trinidad,
Sancti Spíritus
☎ (419) 2180
Restaurant; swimming pool; games room;
rifle range

Hotel Faro de Luna
(27 rooms)
Carretera Pasacaballos, km 18, Playa
Rancho Luna, Cienfuegos
☎ (48) 162, 165 and 168 fax: (48) 33-5059
www.cubanacan.cu
Restaurant and bar; swimming pool; car and
moped rental

Hotel Rancho Luna
(225 rooms)
Carretera a Rancho Luna, km 16, Playa
Rancho Luna, Cienfuegos
☎ (48) 120 fax: (783) 5057
2 restaurants and 5 bars; swimming pool;
store; car and moped rental

Villa Guajimico
(51 rooms)
Carretera de Cienfuegos a Trinidad,
Cienfuegos
☎ (432) 45-1205
Restaurant, bar and café; swimming pool;
car, bike and moped rental; sports equipment rental; tours

Jardines de la Reina

La Tortuga Lodge (the floating hotel)
(8 rooms)
East of Cayo Caballones, Archipiélago de los
Jardines de la Reina, Ciego de Ávila
Booked through: Avalon Dive Center/Press
Tours, S.r.l., Milan, Italy
☎ 39-335-8149111 fax: 39-02-714447
www.avalons.net
avalon@avalons.net
Live-aboard style accommodations on 500-
sq-m converted barge; 8 air conditioned
rooms with private baths accommodate 22
passengers; dock for diving and fishing boats

Santiago de Cuba

Bucanero Hotel
(200 rooms)
Carretera de Baconao, km 4, Arroyo La
Costa, Santiago de Cuba
☎ (226) 69-1446 fax: (226) 8-6108
Restaurants and bar; swimming pool

Farallón de Caribe
(140 rooms)
Carretera de Pilón, km 14, Playa Marea del
Portillo, Pilón, Granma
☎ (23) 59-4032
www.cubanacan.cu
View of Sierra Maestra mountains; swimming
pool; sports equipment rental; car rental;
price includes cocktails and buffet meals

Hotel Balneario del Sol
(123 rooms)
Carretera a Baconao, km 38.5, Baconao,
Santiago de Cuba
☎ (39) 8113
Restaurant and bar; swimming pool

Hotel Marea del Portillo
(70 rooms, 4 suites, 56 bungalows)
Carretera de Pilón, km 14,
Playa Marea del Portillo, Pilón, Granma
☎ (23) 594-2201 and -2203
www.cubanacan.cu
Restaurant and bar; swimming pool; car and
moped rental

SuperClubs Los Galeones
(32 rooms)
Carretera de Chivirico, km 70, Guamá,
Santiago de Cuba
☎ (022) 2-6160 and -6435
www.cubanacan.cu
galeones@smar.scu.cyt.cu
Swimming pool and sauna; balcony; price
includes all meals

SuperClubs Sierra Mar
(200 rooms)
Carretera de Chivirico, km 60, Guamá,
Santiago de Cuba
☎ (022) 2-6337 and -9110 fax: (022) 2-
9116 and -9007
www.cubanacan.cu
sierramar@smar.scu.cyt.cu
Swimming pool; sports equipment rental;
car rental; price includes buffet meals, daily
activities program and non-motorized sports
at the dive shop

Guardalavaca

Hotel Atlántico
(231 rooms, 1 suite)
Playa Guardalavaca, Banes, Holguín
☎ (24) 3-0180 fax: (24) 2-1326
www.cubanacan.cu
Restaurant; swimming pool; sports equipment rental; car rental; tours

Hotel Guardalavaca
(232 rooms)
Playa Guardalavaca, Banes, Holguín
☎ (24) 3-0121 fax: (24) 3-0221
www.cubanacan.cu
Restaurant; disco; swimming pool; car rental; fridge in room

Las Brisas Hotel
(231 rooms)
Calle 2 #2, Playa Guardalavaca, Banes, Holguín
☎ (24) 3-0218 fax: (24) 3-0028
www.cubanacan.cu
Restaurant, café and 3 bars; swimming pool, sports equipment rental; price includes meals

Meliá Río de Oro
(292 rooms, 6 suites, 2 garden villas)
Playa Esmeralda, Carretera Guardalavaca, Aptdo posta 007, Rafael Freyre, Holguín
☎ (24) 3-0090 through -0094
www.solmelia.es
Restaurant and bars; karaoke; swimming pool and sauna; gym; water bikes; sports equipment rental

Santa Lucía

Cuatro Vientos Hotel
(214 rooms)
Playa Santa Lucía, Nuevitas, Camagüey
☎ (32) 33-03142 fax: (32) 33-4533
www.cubanacan.cu
Restaurant; bar; swimming pool; car rental; sports equipment rental

Hotel Club Caracol
(150 rooms, 4 suites)
Playa Santa Lucía, Nuevitas, Camagüey
☎ (32) 33-5043
www.cubanacan.cu
Restaurants and bar; disco; swimming pool; bike and horseback excursions; price includes breakfast

Villa Coral
(246 rooms, 52 suites, 12 bungalows)
Playa Santa Lucía, Nuevitas, Camagüey
☎ (32) 3613
www.cubanacan.cu
Restaurants; sports equipment rental; fridge in room

Cayo Coco

Hotel Tryp Cayo Coco
(485 rooms)
Cayo Coco, Ciego de Ávila
☎ (33) 30-1311 fax (33) 30-1386
www.cubanacan.cu
Restaurant and bar; disco; swimming pool; car, moped and bike rental

Sol Club Cayo Coco
(266 rooms, 4 suites)
Cayo Coco, Ciego de Ávila
☎ (33) 30-1280 fax: (33) 30-1285
www.solmelia.es
solclub.cayococo@melia.solmelia.cma.net
Restaurants and bars; 2 swimming pools; gym; massage; car rental; fridge and hair dryer in room

Villa Cojimar Cayo Guillermo
(80 rooms)
Cayo Guillermo, Ciego de Ávila
☎ (33) 5221 fax: (33) 5554
Restaurant and bar

Varadero

Bella Costa Hotel
(306 rooms)
Avenida de Las Américas, Varadero, Matanzas
☎ (5) 66-7210 fax: (5) 66-7205
www.cubanacan.cu
Restaurant and bar; car rental; sports equipment rental

Club Tropical
(225 rooms)
Av. 1 between Calles 21 and 22, Varadero, Matanzas
☎ (5) 6-3915 fax: (5) 6-7227
Restaurants; swimming pool and gym; private balcony; shops; sports equipment rental

Club Varadero
(98 junior suites, 160 suites)
Carretera Las Américas, km 3, Varadero, Matanzas
☎ (5) 66-7030 and -7031 fax: (5) 66-7005
www.cubanacan.cu
reservas@clubvar.var.cyt.cu
Restaurants and bars; private terrace with view; gym; tennis; sports equipment; price includes all meals and activities

Hotel Internacional
(319 rooms, 2 suites)
Carretera Las Américas, Varadero, Matanzas
☎ (5) 66-7038 fax: (5) 66-7246
3 restaurants and 4 bars; disco; swimming
pool and sauna; moped rental

Sol Club Coral Hotel
(324 rooms)
Avenida de Las Américas and Calle K,
Reparto La Torre, Varadero, Matanzas
☎ (5) 66-7240 fax: (5) 66-7194
www.solmelia.es
solclub.coral@coral.solmelia.cma.net
Restaurants and bars; swimming pool and
gym; sports equipment rental; price is all-
inclusive with buffet meals

Sol Club Las Sirenas Hotel
(310 rooms)
Avenida de Las Américas and Calle K,
Reparto La Torre, Varadero, Matanzas
☎ (5) 66-8070 fax: (5) 66-8075
www.solmelia.es
solclub.lassirenas@sirenas.solmelia.cma.net
Restaurants and bars; karaoke; swimming
pool and gym; sports equipment rental;
price is all-inclusive with buffet meals

Havana Area

Bio Caribe Hotel
(105 rooms, 15 suites)
Calle 158 corner of 31, Playa,
Havana
☎ (7) 33-6839 fax: (7) 33-6839
www.cubanacan.cu
reserva@biocar.cha.cyt.cu
Restaurant and bars; swimming pool;
car rental

El Viejo y El Mar
(186 rooms)
Calle 248 and Av. 5, Santa Fe, Playa,
Havana
☎ (7) 33-6336 fax: (7) 33-6823
www.cubanacan.cu
Restaurants and bars; disco; swimming pool,
sauna and massage; sports equipment
rental; car rental

Jardin del Eden Hotel
(314 rooms)
Calle 248 and Av. 5, Santa Fe, Playa,
Havana
☎ (7) 33-1150 through -1156
fax: (7) 33-1149 and -1536
www.cubanacan.cu
Restaurants and bars; swimming pool;
sports equipment rental; car rental

Marina Hemingway Residential Complexes
(78 bungalows and houses)
Marina Hemingway, Calle 248 and Av. 5,
Santa Fe, Playa, Havana
☎ (7) 29-7907 fax: (7) 24-1149
Restaurant and bar; swimming pool; sports
equipment rental

Villa Cocomar
Carretera Panamericana, km 23, Caimito,
Havana
☎ (680) 5089, 5389 and 3933
fax: (680) 5089
www.cubanacan.cu
Restaurant and bar; swimming pool; massage; car rental

Diving Services

The following diving services are offered by the state-run Cuban companies
Cubamar, Cubanacán, Marlin and Puerto Sol in conjunction with various foreign
dive companies. Boats may be redistributed depending on demand; boats listed
for each dive center are typical of what is found at each location. Dive operators
are normally willing to incorporate diving activities such as cave diving or night
diving into their programs.

Payment can be made in cash. Credit cards or traveler's checks issued through
a non-U.S. bank and not affiliated with American Express are usually (but not
always) accepted.

Certification Agencies

Most diving services offer diver certification classes or use dive guides that are qualified by one or more of the following agencies:

ACUC (American Canadian Underwater Certification)
CMAS (Confédération Mondiale des Activités Subaquatiques)
NASE (National Academy of Scuba Educators)
NAUI (National Association of Underwater Instructors)
PADI (Professional Association of Diving Instructors)
PDIC (Professional Diving Instructors Corporation)

María la Gorda

Diving Center Puerto Sol - María la Gorda
La Bajada, Península de Guanahacabibes,
Sandino, Pinar del Río
☎ (04) 3121 fax: (874) 68368-0520
Certification: ACUC, CMAS
Services: Rental gear
Speciality Dives/Courses: Night diving,
underwater photography, deep diving
Boats: 1 12-passenger (33ft)
Affiliated Hotel: Hotel María la Gorda

Isla de la Juventud

Diving Center Puerto Sol - Hotel Colony
Carretera de Siguanea, km 41,
Isla de la Juventud
☎ (61) 9-8181 fax: (7) 24-5928
Certification: CMAS
Services: Retail and rental gear
Speciality Dives/Courses: Night diving,
underwater photography, wreck diving,
deep diving
Boats: 1 15-passenger (41ft)
Affiliated Hotel: Hotel Colony

Cayo Largo

Diving Center Puerto Sol - Action Sport
Cayo Largo del Sur, Archipiélago de los
Canarreos, Isla de la Juventud
☎/fax: (5) 4-8300
Certification: PADI
Services: Rental gear
Speciality Dives/Courses: Deep diving,
underwater photography, wreck diving,
navigation, search and recovery
Boats: 1 12-passenger (41ft) and
1 24-passenger (44ft)
Affiliated Hotel: none

Diving Center Puerto Sol - Cayo Largo
Cayo Largo del Sur, Archipiélago de los
Canarreos, Isla de la Juventud
☎ (5) 4-8213 fax: (5) 4-8212
Certification: CMAS
Services: Rental gear
Speciality Dives/Courses: Night diving,
underwater photography, deep diving
Boats: 1 15-passenger (41ft)
Affiliated Hotel: none

Playa Girón

Playa Girón Diving Center
Hotel Horizontes Playa Girón,
Peninsula de Zapata, Matanzas
☎ (59) 4118, 4110 and 4195 fax: (59) 4117
Certification: CMAS, ACUC
Services: Rental gear
Speciality Dives/Courses: Shore diving
Boats: none
Affiliated Hotel: Hotel Horizontes
Playa Girón

Octupus Diving Center
Hotel Playa Larga, Peninsula de Zapata,
Matanzas
☎ (59) 7225 and 7219
Certification: CMAS
Services: Rental gear
Speciality Dives/Courses: Shore diving
Boats: none
Affiliated Hotel: Hotel Playa Larga

Cienfuegos, Guajimico & Trinidad

Diving Center Puerto Sol - Cayo Blanco
Península de Ancón, Trinidad, Sancti Spíritus
☎ (41) 9-6205
Certification: CMAS, ACUC
Services: Rental gear
Speciality Dives/Courses: Night diving,
deep diving
Boats: 1 12-passenger (33ft)
Affiliated Hotels: Hotel Ancón,
Hotel Costa Sur

Diving Center Puerto Sol - Whale Shark
Carretera Pasacaballos, km 17, Cienfuegos
☎ (434) 8120 through 8123 fax: (33) 5057
Certification: CMAS, NAUI, PADI
Services: Rental gear
Speciality Dives/Courses: Night diving,
deep diving, cave diving
Boats: 1 20-passenger and 1 30-passenger
Affiliated Hotel: Hotel Rancho Luna

Faro de Luna Diving Center
Carretera Pasacaballos, km 18,
Playa Rancho Luna, Cienfuegos
☎ (432) 45-1340 fax: (432) 33-5059
Certification: ACUC
Services: Rental gear
Boats: 2 8-passenger
Affiliated Hotel: Hotel Faro de Luna

Guajimico Diving Center
Carretera de Cienfuegos a Trinidad,
km 42, Guajimico, Cienfuegos
☎ (43) 2-8125
Certification: CMAS
Services: Equipment provided as part of
dive package
Boats: 1 15-passenger (42ft) and
1 22-passenger (39ft)
Affiliated Hotel: Villa Guajimico

Jardines de la Reina

**Diving Center Puerto Sol -
Azulmar/Avalon Dive Center**
Archipiélago Jardines de la Reina, Júcaro,
Ciego de Ávila
☎ (33) 9-8126 fax: (33) 9-8104
Certification: CMAS
Services: Rental gear
Speciality Dives/Courses: Night diving,
deep diving, underwater videography
Boats: 1 15-passenger, 2 10-passenger and
1 6-passenger
Affiliated Hotel: La Tortuga Lodge

Santiago de Cuba

Albacora Diving Center
Playa Marea del Portillo, Pilón, Granma
☎ /fax: (7) 33-5301
Certification: ACUC
Services: Rental gear
Boats: 2 8-passenger
Affiliated Hotels: Farallón del Caribe,
Hotel Marea del Portillo

Bucanero Diving Center
Bucanero Hotel, Carretara de Baconao, km
4, Arroyo La Costa, Santiago de Cuba
☎ (226) 69-1446 fax: (226) 8-6108
Certification: ACUC
Services: Rental gear
Boats: 2 8-passenger
Affiliated Hotel: Bucanero Hotel

Sierra Mar Diving Center
SuperClubs Sierra Mar, Carretera de
Chivirico, km 60, Guamá, Santiago de Cuba
☎ (226) 2-6436
Certification: ACUC
Services: Rental gear
Boats: 2 8-passenger
Affiliated Hotel: SuperClubs Sierra Mar

Sigua Diving Center
Carretera de Baconao, km 25, Playa Sigua,
Santiago de Cuba
☎ (226) 9-1446 fax: (226) 8-6108
Certification: ACUC
Services: Rental gear
Boats: 2 8-passenger
Affiliated Hotel: Hotel Balneario del Sol

Guardalavaca

Eagle Ray
Playa Guardalavaca, Holguín
☎ (24) 33-6702 and -6041
fax: (24) 30-6323
Certification: ACUC
Services: Rental gear
Boats: 2 8-passenger
Affiliated Hotel: Hotel Atlántico

Santa Lucía

Sharks Friends Diving Center
Hotel Cuatro Vientos, Playa Santa Lucía,
Camagüey
☎ (32) 36-5294 fax: (32) 36-5262
Certification: ACUC
Services: Rental gear
Boats: 2 8-passenger
Affiliated Hotel: Cuatro Vientos Hotel

Cayo Coco

Coco Diving Center
Hotel Tryp, Cayo Coco, Ciego de Ávila
☎ (33) 30-1323
Certification: ACUC
Services: Rental gear
Boats: 2 8-passenger
Affiliated Hotel: Hotel Tryp Cayo Coco

Diving Center Puerto Sol - Cayo Guillermo
Cayo Guillermo, Morón, Ciego de Ávila
☎ (33) 30-1738 fax: (33) 30-1737
Certification: CMAS, ACUC
Services: Rental gear
Speciality Dives/Courses: Night diving, deep diving
Boats: 1 15-passenger (41ft)
Affiliated Hotel: Villa Cojimar Cayo Guillermo

Varadero

Barracuda Diving Center
Av. 1 and Playa, between 59 and 60, Varadero, Matanzas
☎ (5) 16-3481 fax: (5) 66-7072
www.cuba.tc/CubaScuba_VaraderoE
Certification: ACUC
Services: Rental gear
Boats: 2 8-passenger
Affiliated Hotel: Bella Costa Hotel
(The Barracuda dive base also has some accommodations)

Gaviota Diving Center
Punta de Hicacos, Varadero, Matanzas
☎ (5) 66-7755 fax: (5) 66-7756
Certification: CMAS
Services: Rental gear
Boats: 1 12-passenger and 2 20-passenger
Affiliated Hotel: none

Marina Acua Diving Center
Av. Kawama, between Calle 2 and 3, Varadero, Matanzas
☎ (5) 66-8064 fax: (5) 66-7456
Certification: PADI, NAUI, CMAS
Services: Rental gear
Speciality Dives/Courses: Cave diving, deep diving, nitrox
Boats: 1 20-passenger (50ft)
Affiliated Hotel: none

SuperClubs Diving Center
Carretera de las Americas, Varadero, Matanzas

☎ (5) 66-7031 fax: (5) 66-7005
Certification: CMAS
Services: Rental gear
Boats: 2 10-passenger
Affiliated Hotel: Club Varadero

Havana Area

Caribbean Diving Center Puerto Sol
Via Blanca, km 19, Residencial Tarará, Marina Tarará, Habana del Este, Ciudad de la Habana
☎ /fax: (7) 97-1462
www.webatwork.net/caribbean_spa
psoldiv@psoldiv.get.cma.net
Certification: CMAS, NASE
Services: Rental gear, dive trips to other Cuban dive regions
Speciality Dives/Courses: Night diving, cave diving, deep diving
Boats: 1 12-passenger (33ft)
Affiliated Hotel: none

Cocosub Diving Center
Carretera Panamericana, km 23.5, Caimito, Havana
☎ (7) 80-5389 and -3933 fax: (7) 80-5089
Certification: ACUC
Services: Rental gear
Boats: 1 10-passenger
Affiliated Hotel: none

Diving World - Horizontes (Manotour)
Cayo Levisa, La Palma, Pinar del Río
☎ (7) 24-1162 and -1165
Certification: PDIC, CMAS
Boats: 2 10-passenger
Affiliated Hotel: none

La Aguja/Blue Reef Diving Center
Villa Cocomar Hotel, Carretera Panamericana, km 23, Caimito, Havana
☎ (7) 29-7201 fax: (7) 24-1149
Certification: ACUC
Services: Rental gear
Boats: 2 8-passenger
Affiliated Hotel: Villa Cocomar

Live-Aboards

El Boca del Torro
Contact info: Trisub, Rue Longue Vie, 43 B-1050, Brussels, Belgium
☎ 32-2-511-02-36 fax: 32-2-511-50-28
Home port: Trinidad
Description: 25m boat

Accommodations: 5 cabins - 3 twin, 1 quad and 1 double
Destinations: Trinidad to Jardines de la Reina
Duration: 6-night trips
Season: Year-round
Passengers: 11

Explorador
Contact info: Avalon Dive Center/Press Tours S.r.l., Milan, Italy
☎ 39-335-8149111 fax: 39-02-714447
www.avalons.net
avalon@avalons.net
Home port: Júcaro
Description: 19m boat
Accommodations: 4 double cabins
Destinations: Natural Park of Los Jardines de la Reina
Duration: 6-night trips
Season: Year-round
Passengers: 8

Halcón
Contact info: Avalon Dive Center/Press Tours S.r.l., Milan, Italy
☎ 39-33-8149111 fax: 39-02-714447
www.avalons.net
avalon@avalons.net
Home port: Júcaro
Description: 25m boat
Accommodations: 6 double cabins
Destinations: Natural Park of Los Jardines de la Reina
Duration: 6-night trips
Season: Year-round
Passengers: 12

Dive-Package Companies

Dive packages normally include flights, transfers, accommodations and a specified number of dives. Some companies can incorporate on-land sightseeing into your package. The following represent just a few of the operators that offer diving trips and packages.

Cuba Travel
Contact info: Av. Quintana Roo 1621, Suite TIJ 1173, Zona Centro, Tijuana B.C., 22000 Mexico **or** 4492 Camino de la Plaza, Suite TIJ-1773, San Diego, CA 92173-3097, USA
☎ 011-526-686-6298 or U.S. voice mail 310-842-4148
www.havanacuba.com
scuba@havanacuba.com
Description: Mexico-based tour operator offering pre-paid dive tours to Cuba
Accommodations: Havana Libre, Hotel Colony and Hotel Ancón
Destinations: Isla de la Juventud, María la Gorda, Playa Larga, Trinidad and Marina Tarará (Havana)
Season: Year-round

Estiber
Contact info: Casanova 100, 08011 Barcelona, Spain
☎ 93-454-83-08 fax: 93-451-12-23
www.estiber.com
Description: Spanish tour operator offering 5-day pre-paid dive tours to Cuba
Accommodations: Hotel Colony and Hotel María la Gorda
Destinations: Isla de la Juventud and María la Gorda
Season: Consult with company

Regal Holidays
Contact info: 22 High Street, Sutton, Ely, Cambridgeshire, CB6 2RB, UK
☎ 01-353-778096 fax: 01-353-777897
www.regal-diving.co.uk
andy@regal-diving.co.com
Description: U.K.-based tour operator offering sightseeing and dive tours
Accommodations: Hotel Colony and Hotel María la Gorda
Destinations: María la Gorda, Isla de la Juventud and Trinidad
Season: Year-round

Scubacan International
Contact info: 1365 Yonge St., Suite 208, Toronto, Ontario Canada M4T 2P7
☎ 888-799-CUBA fax: 416-927-1257
www.scubacan.com
info@scubacan.com
Description: Canada-based dive tour operator offering pre-paid, "fully hosted" tours to Cuba and Cuban Treasure Hunting specialty tours. Specialize in bringing U.S. tourists to Cuba.
Accommodations: Hotel Colony
Destination: Isla de la Juventud
Season: Year-round

Scuba en Cuba
Contact info: 7 Maybank Gardens, Pinner,
Middlesex, HA5 2JW, UK
☎ 44-01895-624100
fax: 44-01895-624377
www.scuba-en-cuba.com
Diana_W_scubaenc@compuserve.com
Description: U.K.-based dive tour operator
offering package and tailor-made
dive tours to Cuba

Accommodations: Throughout Cuba
Destinations: Maria la Gorda, Isla de la
Juventud, Jardines de la Reina,
Cienfuegos, Trinidad, Guajimico,
Cayo Largo, Havana, Guardalavaca,
Varadero and other sites on request
Season: Year-round

Tourist Offices

In Cuba

Many visitors to Cuba are part of a packaged tour that provides them with customized information. There are almost no general tourist information offices for individual travelers in Cuba. State-run travel agencies, such as Havanatur and Rumbos, are found in the main tourist centers. They book accommodations, rental vehicles, sightseeing tours, flights and so on—they have little or no information on dive-specific or alternative money-saving possibilities.

Abroad

Cuba has an extensive network of tourism promotion offices overseas that are excellent sources of free brochures and information.

Other Cuban travel companies with offices around the world include the government hotel corporation Cubanacán (they have offices worldwide that provide information about their hotels and sell Cuban travel videos, but don't book tours or reserve rooms) and the Cuban airline Cubana de Aviación, both potential sources of useful information.

Argentina: Cuban Tourist Board
Paraguay No 631, 2do piso A, Buenos Aires
☎ 54-1-311-4198

Canada: Bureau de Tourisme de Cuba
440 Boulevard René Lévesque Ouest,
Bureau 1402, Montreal, Quebec H2Z 1V7
☎ 514-857-8004 fax: 514-875-8006

Canada: Cuban Tourist Board
55 Queen St. East, Suite 705,
Toronto, Ontario M5C 1R6
☎ 416-362-0700 fax: 416-362-6799

France: Office de Tourisme de Cuba
280 Boulevard Raspael, Paris 75014
☎ 33-01-4538-9010 fax: 33-01-4538-9930

Germany: Cuban Tourist Board
An der Hauptwache 7, 60313
Frankfurt/Main
☎ 49-69-288-322 fax: 49-69-296-664

**Italy: Ufficio di Promozione ed
Informazione Turistica di Cuba**
Via General Fara 30, terzo piano,
Milano 20124
☎ 39-2-6698-1463 fax: 39-2-669-0042

Mexico: Cuban Tourist Board
Insurgentes Sur No 421, Complejo Aristos,
Edificio B, Local 310, Mexico City 06100, DF
☎ 52-5-574-9454

Netherlands: Cuban Tourist Board
Jan van Gentstraat 130, 1171 GN
Badhoevedorp
☎ 31-20-659-9271 fax: 31-20-659-9218

**Spain: Oficina de Promoción e
Información Turística de Cuba**
Paseo de La Habana 27, Madrid 28036
☎ 34-1-411-3097 fax: 34-1-564-5804

Index

dive sites covered in this book appear in **bold** type

Lonely Planet Pisces Books

The **Diving & Snorkeling** books are dive guides to top destinations worldwide. Beautifully illustrated with full-color photos throughout, the series explores the best diving and snorkeling areas and prepares divers for what to expect when they get there. Each site is described in detail, with information on suggested ability levels, depth, visibility and, of course, marine life. There's basic topside information as well for each destination. Don't miss the guides to:

Australia's Great Barrier Reef
Australia: Southeast Coast
Bahamas: Family Islands
& Grand Bahama
Bahamas: Nassau &
New Providence
Baja California
Bali & the Komodo Region
Belize
Bermuda
Bonaire
British Virgin Islands
Cayman Islands
Cocos Island
Cozumel
Cuba
Curaçao
Dominica
Fiji
Florida Keys
Guam & Yap

Hawaiian Islands
Jamaica
Northern California &
Monterey Peninsula
Pacific Northwest
Palau
Papua New Guinea
Puerto Rico
Red Sea
Roatan & Honduras'
Bay Islands
Scotland
Seychelles
Southern California
St. Maarten, Saba,
& St. Eustatius
Texas
Truk Lagoon
Turks & Caicos
U.S. Virgin Islands
Vanuatu

Plus illustrated natural history guides:

Pisces Guide to Caribbean Reef Ecology
Great Reefs of the World
Sharks of Tropical & Temperate Seas
Venomous & Toxic Marine Life of the World
Watching Fishes